DISASTERS
of
ATLANTIC CANADA

Stories of Courage & Chaos

Vernon Oickle

FOLK
LORE
PUBLISHING

The Publisher: Folklore Publishing
Website: www.folklorepublishing.com

Library and Archives Canada Cataloguing in Publication

Oickle, Vernon, 1961–
    Disasters of Atlantic Canada : Stories of Courage & Chaos / Vernon Oickle

Includes bibliographical references.
ISBN 13: 978-1-894864-15-2
ISBN 10: 1-894864-15-8

    1. Disasters—Atlantic Canada—History. 2. Atlantic Canada—History—Miscellanea. I. Title.

F1035.8.A27.2007   971   C2007-901876-9

Project Director: Faye Boer
Proofreader: Bridget Stirling
Production: Michael Cooke, Willa Kung
Cover Image: Andres Wertheim/Deepol/plainpicture/Jupiter images

Photography credits: Every effort has been made to accurately credit the sources of photographs. Any errors or omissions should be reported directly to the publisher for correction in future editions. Photographs courtesy of Brian Bursey (p. 105); Canada Department of Energy, Mines and Resources (p.157, 1970-018); Canada Department of National Defense/Library & Archives (p. 145, 1964-114); Collections Canada (p.47, 1986-56-260); p. 158, PA-028843); Flicker.com (p. 53); Government of Nova Scotia (p. 138, N-138); Lighthouse Publishing Ltd. (p. 36; p. 216; p. 223; p. 225); National Archives of Canada (p. 178, 1977-286) Photos.com (cover; p. 49; p. 116); Wikipedia (p. 140)

We acknowledge the support of the Alberta Foundation for the Arts for our publishing program. We acknowledge the financial support of the Government of Canada through the Book Publishing Industry Development Program (BPIDP) for our publishing activities.

Canadian   Patrimoine
Heritage   canadien

PC:P5

Table of Contents

Dedication

DEDICATED TO THE MEMORIES of those who died in these tragedies and to those brave men and women who answered the call to help despite great risk to their own lives.

Acknowledgements

I WOULD LIKE TO ACKNOWLEDGE and thank all those who provided assistance to make this book a reality, particularly those who work in the various museums throughout Atlantic Canada and those who dedicate their lives to preserving history and educating us about the many unfortunate disasters that have gripped this part of the country. You will meet each of them by name as you read the following text. I would also like to extend a special note of gratitude to family members of victims for graciously sharing their stories and to survivors who imparted their vivid and often painful memories from these tragic events. As well, a note of thanks to those who talked about the brave rescue efforts undertaken to assist those touched by the following disasters.

I must extend a special note of thanks to reporter Lisa Brown from Lighthouse Publishing in Bridgewater, Nova Scotia, for her assistance with the Swissair crash story and to Paul Banks at the Gander *Beacon* in Newfoundland for his help with the Arrow Air plane crash disaster. Their attention to detail and accuracy in reporting have proven invaluable in this effort. And a note of gratitude to the staff of Folklore Publishing, particularly Faye Boer, for giving me the opportunity to write this book, and to my editor for his excellent guidance.

And no thank-you list for this book would be complete without the name of Patrick Hirtle. Let's just say this project would not have been a reality without his assistance. He is an extraordinary researcher who has earned my utmost respect.

Finally, deepest, heartfelt thanks for my family—Nancy, Kellen and Colby—for their love and understanding. Without their support throughout the researching and writing of this book, the project would not have been possible.

Introduction

WHO WOULD THINK THAT community newspaper reporters in rural communities on the picturesque and tranquil coast of Nova Scotia would be writing about a tragic plane crash that left 229 people dead? Who would think that residents of the normally peaceful South Shore region of Nova Scotia would be dealing with such a horrific accident that it left them stunned beyond belief? As the editor of two weekly publications based in the town of Bridgewater, Nova Scotia, I found it difficult to comprehend the events then, and, even today, when thinking about the images we encountered, I still find it difficult to keep it all in perspective.

It is hard to believe, yet there we were in the days and weeks of September 1998 following the crash of Swissair Flight 111, the doomed jetliner that plunged into the choppy waters of Peggy's Cove around 10:30 that Wednesday night. It was a surreal image. Such terrible accidents were not supposed to happen in our piece of the world, yet we know tragedy can strike at any time and anywhere. No place is immune. A look through the history of Atlantic Canada reveals a landscape cluttered with disasters. Whether resulting from human error or natural causes or other circumstances beyond human control, all have left a legacy of death and destruction.

Nevertheless, no one ever expects to be thrust into the middle of a catastrophic event. Nova Scotians hear about such disasters all the time. They happen to other people in other places. They are not supposed to happen in our own backyard, but we know they can. We've seen it. We've experienced them many times. For me, the events began shortly before 11:00 PM on September 2, 1998, when I received a call from one of the reporters I worked with at Lighthouse Publishing, the company that publishes our newspapers. It was a dark, dreary and foggy night. My colleague told me that he had just received a phone call and was on his way to a plane crash reported to have occurred somewhere in the Blandford area, near the world-famous tourist destination of Peggy's Cove. He had no details, but he understood the aircraft was carrying around 100 people. In the hours that followed, we learned the number of people on board was much higher.

Today, after having worked for more than 25 years in the community newspaper business, I am seldom surprised by what I hear when I answer the phone. However, I was not prepared for that call on that night. My first reaction was to dismiss the report, foolishly thinking such a thing could never happen here in our part of the world. After all, this is Nova Scotia. Then reality sank in. If he had been notified of an accident, it must be true, and, as the editor of those papers, I had a job to do. After shaking the cobwebs from my head, I called other staff members to work on the story and dispatched a second reporter to what we believed was the scene of the crash. At that time, we still had no idea of the magnitude of the tragedy that had just occurred in our midst.

As those two reporters followed emergency personnel along the South Shore to Bayswater Beach and then to Peggy's Cove, I maintained an all-night vigil in front of the television and worked the phones, trying to piece together a picture of the disaster. According to reports that emerged throughout the night, emergency personnel from all over Nova Scotia, but particularly those along the South Shore, responded in a professional manner, their utmost concern being for the people on board the ill-fated jetliner. Besides emergency crews dispatched to the crash scene, individuals from throughout the province responded to the news, hoping to assist in some small way, willing to do anything they could to alleviate the strain and burden on local rescuers. Of particular note were the hundreds of residents from the many villages along the coast who quickly reached out to help in whatever way they could, even if it was just making a Thermos of coffee for rescue personnel facing a long, damp night or bringing blankets down to the shore in case survivors were brought in from the chilly Atlantic waters. At this point, hopes were still high that survivors would be found.

As the hours passed, and it became painfully obvious that the rescue effort would become a recovery operation, anxiety turned to sorrow. By dawn the next morning, officials confirmed that all onboard had perished when the aircraft ditched into the unforgiving Atlantic Ocean. As the day wore on, we became distraught to think so many people—even though they were strangers—had lost their lives in our backyard. How could this happen, we wondered. Why here?

The people of the South Shore have endured many tragedies over the years. Each has its own special place in our memories and our hearts. The loss of human life is always hard to accept. This tragedy, like so many others, offered few answers to our many questions. Before that deadly September, whenever local emergency personnel held mock disasters and prepared for such a calamity, we told ourselves such things would never happen here. Sadly, we now know such tragedies can and will happen in our midst. Disasters know no geographical boundaries. The serenity of our world was changed forever by this tragic crash.

As our staff scrambled to meet the challenges of this story, I couldn't stop thinking about the people on board that flight. Obviously, they knew their plane was in trouble. What were they thinking as the reality of their plight sank in? What were they doing during the last few minutes of their lives just before the crash? Were they praying for help and asking why their prayers weren't being answered? It doesn't matter that we didn't know them, because people are just people, no matter who they are or where they live. The reality is that 229 people plunged to their death that Wednesday night, taking all their hopes and dreams with them. Everything else pales in comparison.

In the aftermath of the disaster, media from around the world converged on the South Shore. As the community paper, we were right there with them because this was as much a local story as it was an international event. Admittedly, it was often a challenge. Members of the *Lighthouse* editorial staff experienced sights, sounds and emotional sensations that left us numb beyond description and hanging our heads in disbelief. The toll of this air disaster cannot be measured only by the passenger list and crew roster. Although it devastated the lives of the victims' families and friends, it also had a long-term emotional impact on the residents of these South Shore communities. An army of volunteers unselfishly extended a helping hand. Brave fishermen immediately sprang into action after the crash in a valiant attempt to rescue any survivors—and they stayed on to help in the recovery effort. Others, such as the volunteer firefighters, search crews, police officers and all the recovery personnel will also continue to suffer from the stress associated with the crash for years to come.

In dealing with the plane disaster, the emotions of everyone connected with the tragedy were stretched to the breaking point as we tried to cope with such a terrible loss of life. As reporters covering the tragedy, we always tried to be sensitive, but, as sometimes happens with such a story, the truth may have seemed sensational, particularly to observers on the outside critiquing everything we did. Did we cross the line with this story? I don't think so. We considered every item as we dealt with it. This was a heart-wrenching story. By its very nature, it demanded close attention to all the details. Although we may have wanted to make the story more palatable, there comes a point where it is necessary to relate the facts so that we can all fully understand the tragedy. Yes, some people may have found some of the details offensive or distasteful. As reporters, we also found them shocking, but we believed the story must be told. It is impossible to cover an event of such destruction and death without revealing some intimate details.

There were times in the days following September 2, 1998, that we all felt overwhelmed by the details, but we also knew the public deserved to be kept fully informed. So we pushed forward. We were careful not to spoonfeed only the less "sensational" facts to the public. People needed to know the whole truth about such a tragedy. Some things get in your head and stay there. This is one of those things. This tragedy left behind many heart-wrenching images. In the days that followed, I saw one young woman, a grieving family member, pass her infant to a man standing next to her and then try to throw herself into the cold Atlantic near the Peggy's Cove lighthouse. And I will never forget the tortured cries of an elderly family member screaming, "My God! My God!" as he was carried away by stretcher. He had collapsed on the rocky shore while visiting the site not far from where his loved ones had died.

Above all, the sights and sounds of the memorial services that followed the crash are forever fixed in my mind and heart. I cannot erase the images of mothers, fathers, wives, husbands, sisters, brothers, sons and daughters, crying over their terrible loss as the list of names of those who died in the crash was read. Anyone who shared this experience will understand the anguish one feels when confronted by such grief. If these sights have left such an indelible mark on me, I cannot begin to imagine what people more closely associated with the recovery of crash victims must have felt. Surely, their lives will never be the same again.

As I stood in the crowd at the memorial service a week after the terrible tragedy occurred, I found myself glancing skywards hoping for some inner strength that would anchor me in this angry sea of emotion. Ironically, just before the service began, I was shocked back to reality by a jet passing overhead, its stream of spent fuel slowly tailing off and its passengers oblivious to the solemn crowd gathered below. And there it was. In one quick glance, the truth was driven home to me, and I was left with an eerie, unsettling feeling. Whatever the tragedy, the world does keep on spinning. The challenge facing everyone touched by the crash of Flight 111 was to hang on, even when it felt like they were falling off.

The disasters chosen for inclusion in this book were selected for several reasons. Some, such as the sinking of the *Ocean Ranger* oil rig, the Halifax Explosion, the sinking of the *Titanic*, the crash of Swissair Flight 111, the twin Springhill mining disasters, the Arrow Air plane crash in Newfoundland and the Westray Coal Mine Explosion, were a natural fit. All the disasters found herein, however, even those that are not as well known, have much in common. They all represent loss of property, and, in most cases, the loss of human life. But beyond that, the stories are also about the people who responded to the emergencies, those who demonstrated true courage while risking their own life and limbs.

Throughout the stories that you will read in the following pages, a common theme emerges: in the face of seemingly insurmountable odds, people will always rise to the challenge. Despite possible harm to themselves, people will reach out to help someone in trouble. That has always been the case in Atlantic Canada. This book is about the many disasters that have occurred in Atlantic Canada in the past two centuries and about the loss of life and human suffering that come with such catastrophic events. But it is also as much about the human spirit and the will to persevere, to overcome the obstacles, to beat the odds. We see that two types of catastrophes can occur, one type at the hand of human beings, the other through natural forces. In both cases, however, the loss of human life and the suffering of the untold thousands of people can often be staggering. The price of these disasters is paid not only in dollars — it is also paid in human lives and spilled blood. But it is the ability of a community to survive that is the real story. You will discover that reality throughout this book.

In thinking about the impacts that such disasters ultimately have on communities where tragedies occur, I am reminded of the words of Transportation Safety Board chairman Camille Thériault on March 27, 2003, in thanking the people of Nova Scotia who responded to the crash of Swissair Flight 111, particularly those in communities surrounding the crash site:

> *"In the darkest days, you provided comfort where there was only pain; compassion where there was only suffering; hope where there was only despair. Thank you for showing the world the very best of our national character."*

Thériault could have been speaking about any community in Atlantic Canada in response to any one of the following tragedies.

Part I
Natural Disasters

Yankee Gale

October 3, 1851
The Atlantic Ocean, off the north shore of PEI

EARLY IN OCTOBER 1851, still 16 years before Confederation, a large fleet of fishing vessels moved close along the coastline following schools of mackerel into the shallow water off the northern shore of Prince Edward Island. In this era, long before the modern age of overfishing by the large freezer trawlers in the latter part of the 20th century, the fish were plentiful. The ocean's bounty was the mainstay of the island economy, as it was in the entire Atlantic region.

More than 100 schooners were on the waters that day, many of them crewed by American sailors—or "Yankees"—from New England ports. Suddenly, an unexpected gale blew in from the northeast. Without the advance warning provided by today's electronic instruments, the boats were open targets. They were helpless: nowhere to run and nowhere to take cover from nature's force. Under the massive seas and hurricane-force winds, the vessels were tossed about on the mountainous waves. Many boats were smashed against the rocky shoals. The aftermath of the powerful storm was catastrophic.

In total, historical data suggests that the storm left between 80 and 120 ships in smashed ruins. Conflicting sources give differing counts of the dead, but it is believed that, by the time the storm subsided, it had claimed as many as 160 to 220 fishermen. Without accurate records, however, it is impossible to say for sure how many men died because of the killer storm. Some records even suggest that as many as 400 men were lost. Although the exact death count may be a mystery, the Yankee Gale, which was named for the large number of Americans killed, still goes down in the annals of history as one of the deadliest storms on record in Atlantic Canada.

Most of the dead were lost at sea, their remains never found. However, some bodies were eventually relinquished by the Atlantic. Those that were found were recovered and subsequently buried in several cemeteries on Prince Edward Island's north shore.

October 3, 1851, may be in the books as the date of the worst disaster in Prince Edward Island history, but it was also the date when the true spirit of heroism was amply evident. In true Maritime fashion, the residents of Prince Edward Island flocked to the shores to rescue survivors and to claim the dead. Many of the bodies of the sailors that washed ashore were never identified—such as the 12 who were discovered at Cavendish Beach—but they were treated with the ultimate respect they deserved. Today, the shoreline cliffs of Prince Edward Island are festooned with small graveyards overlooking the sea and containing the remains of men who succumbed to its mighty force. Most of those graves contain the unidentified remains of sailors who perished in the Yankee Gale.

Although there is very little information on the identity of the sailors and fishermen interred there, the Yankee Hill–French River Cemetery is said to be the final resting place for at least 25 American sailors who perished in the Yankee Gale.

A project to restore the historic cemetery was completed in 2002. The work, which involved removing overgrowth and building a bridge, was done by community groups working together with the Departments of Fisheries, Aquaculture and Environment, Transportation and Public Works and the Community and Correctional Services Division of the Office of the Attorney General. In addition, members of the team researched the genealogy of any names found on headstones.

The person who spearheaded this joint project, Grace MacLeod of the Coronation Women's Institute, expressed her satisfaction by saying:

> *"We are so pleased with the work that has been put into this restoration project resulting in a cemetery that truly reflects the history of the area and honours the individuals who rest here."*

Today, thanks to such community-based efforts, memories of this terrible tragedy have been assured their place in the annals of the island's storied history.

Saxby Gale

October 4 and 5, 1869
The Gaspé Peninsula, New Brunswick

ACCORDING TO the Canadian Hurricane Centre, a branch of Environment Canada, the Saxby Gale took place on October 4 and 5, 1869. The storm was named for Lieutenant Stephen Martin Saxby, an instructor in the British Royal Navy. One year earlier, he purportedly predicted that a major weather system, in conjunction with an extreme tide, would wreak havoc somewhere on earth within the next calendar year.

Environment Canada surmises that Saxby must have recognized that on October 5, 1869, the moon would make an especially close pass to the Earth, and in combination with the new moon phase, the result would be exaggerated tides. An atypically high tide combined with a severe weather system would be a recipe for a flooding disaster. Saxby wrote numerous letters to London's the *Standard* newspaper, as much as a year in advance, warning of the potential disaster that could be caused by unusually high tides on October 5, 1869.

Ironically, one of Saxby's warnings was picked up in the Maritimes just days before the storm. On October 1, 1869, the *Halifax Evening Express* printed a note from local amateur meteorologist Frederick Allison, who took the time to relay Saxby's prediction in his monthly weather column. But, without the modern meteorological tools of today, neither Saxby in England nor anyone else could predict a precise locale most likely to be affected by the surging tides.

Unfortunately, no one knew at the time that a powerful storm had formed off the coast of the Carolinas and that it was rapidly tracking to the northeast, so few Atlantic Canadians were prepared for the weather phenomenon— of which New Brunswick bore the brunt—despite Saxby's scientifically founded prediction.

The wind began in the afternoon of October 4 across much of the Maritimes, increasing to a gale, with rain beginning right around the supper hour. By 8:30 PM, the wind had reached hurricane force, climbing to its maximum intensity by 9:00 PM. As the storm began to pass through the region, the wind swung around to the southwest and began to lose its strength.

The storm actually made landfall in Maine, and, according to United States National Oceanic and Atmospheric Administration weather charts, it tracked across Maine towards northern New Brunswick before losing its equivalent of post-tropical storm status around the Gaspé Peninsula, along the Québec–New Brunswick border. At its peak, the highest sustained winds were reputed to be about 170 kilometres per hour. It was the final storm of the 1869 Atlantic hurricane season.

As damaging as the wind was in some districts, it was the storm surge caused by the combination of severe weather combined with the phase and position of the moon that wrought the most havoc. Moncton reported that the tide rose roughly 2 metres above former record high marks. Dykes throughout the Maritimes, and in particular the Tantramar Marshes and Minas Basin regions, were breached, flooding farmland throughout the region. Although no definite count is possible, it is believed that more than 100 people in the United States and Canada perished during the Saxby Gale.

In St. Andrews, New Brunswick, it was reported that a total of 123 vessels had been beached by the gale. On the opposite Bay of Fundy shore, at Grand Pré, the Horton Dyke gave way, flooding over 1200 hectares, drowning hundreds of cattle in the process. The Windsor Baptist Church was reputed to have had over 2 metres of water in its vestry. In the neighbouring state of Maine, the city of Calais reported significant damage as well, with as many as 120 boats found tossed up on land once the tides had receded.

The St. John *Daily Telegraph* published the following information on the Saxby Gale on October 5, 1869:

THE PREDICTED STORM

At an early hour yesterday the strange sultriness of the atmosphere and the extraordinary heat of the sun, when it shone forth, where remarked by everyone. The barometer fell, and gradually the wind, which was from the South, rose. At 5:00 o'clock PM, *the electric wires to the west of the St. John office were all down, the storm having reached Boston at an early hour of the day. a few hours later eastern wires were blown down, and St. John was cut off from telegraph communication with the rest of the world. In the meantime the wind was getting higher. Soon after 7:00* PM *a heavy storm of rain commenced, but the winds continued as high as ever. Old houses, sheds, gates and light and loose materials of all kinds were subjected to an extraordinary degree of shaking. The howling of the wind along the wharves and among the shipping, the creaking of loose materials, and the cries of sailors and others in cheering each other on in their work or giving directions what to do, produced a good deal of excitement among pedestrians. These manifestations seemed to sustain Captain Saxby's predictions, and were exactly in accordance with the remarks of Mr. Frederick Allison, of Halifax, in commenting on Captain Saxby's predictions.*

With the exception of Friday morning the 1st inst., the wind has been South West since Wednesday, the 20th. In blew rather strongly on Saturday night, but the gale which was at its height between 8:00 and 9:00 PM yesterday, became at last terrific. The sky was cloudy during the day and the motion of clouds from the South. The morning came in foggy, but it soon cleared off and became quite warm. The cirrus, which is the highest cloud, appeared to have been impelled by a West wind. In the afternoon, between 3:00 and 5:00, the clouding became much more dense, and at 6:00, when the four winds of heaven seemed to be gathering their force, it began to rain.

The means of daily barometric readings last week will be seen in our "Weather Report." On Sunday the column fell steadily from 30.120 [inches of mercury, equivalent to 101.98 kilopascals] *to 30.004* [101.59 kilopascals]. *Yesterday the depression was much more rapid, as will be seen by the following figures*

8:00 AM	*29.923* [101.32 kilopascals]
2:00 PM	*29.780*
6:00 PM	*29.527*
8:00 PM	*29.322*
9:00 PM	*29.332*
10:00 PM	*29.375* [99.46 kilopascals]

Thus it will be seen that the atmospheric pressure decreased rapidly during the afternoon until about 8 o'clock, after which it began to increase, losing during the day .591 [2.00 kilopascals] *or nearly 6-tenths of an inch.*

CAPTAIN FRITH'S OBSERVATIONS

Captain Frith, who kept a close eye on five barometers from 10:40 AM (yesterday) to 10:40 PM, went out before 5:00 and advised all the shipmasters in port of the approaching storm. Some heeded his warning; and others, to their subsequent regret, disregarded it. The mean decline of the five barometers from 10:40 AM to 9 PM was .37 [1.25 kilopascals] *and from that hour to 10:40 PM the mean rise amounted to .15* [0.51 kilopascals].

DETAILS AND INCIDENTS

At 7:30 the Carlton Ferry Boat had to stop running as, from the strong tide and ground sea which came rolling in, it was thought prudent to tie-up and avoid running unnecessary risks. People gathered on the wharf of the Empress at an early hour in expectation of her arrival from Annapolis and Digby; but it is hoped that Captain Steen has had the prudence to stay at the other side of the Bay. General Doyle was expected among her passengers. About 8:00, ships Ansel *and* Twilight *broke loose from the Custom House wharf and, drifting a distance to leeward, came in contact with a new ship,* Armanila, *at Lawton's wharf. The water, in the meantime had begun making its way over the wharves, and gradually the heavy sea commenced its work of destruction. The Slips* [at] *lower Cove are more or less wrecked. At Maxwell's Lumber Wharf, the schooner* S.B. Coonhan, *which had both anchors to windward, broke adrift and came surging down upon the wharf.*

The lumber piles were rocking and creaking, and the wharf itself was completely submerged. Some 20 men got out upon the floating lumber, and a fast was landed and held by them while Captain William Robertson and four men were safely landed, the vessel being left to the mercy of the elements with her stern, now high up in the air, and then down among the ground up timber and general wreck around. The pilot boat Circe *got in snug quarters of the Reed's Point wharf, over which the waves dashed in their fury, tearing up the planks and driving them along midway between the Anchor Line warehouse and the International Line floats. Around the Anchor*

Line buildings, the sea dashed furiously and the whole wharf seemed afloat. On the International Line wharf, planks were torn up and quite large quantity of coal lying loose was washed overboard or spread over the face of wharf. The barque Vortex and the ship Beacon Light, which were to leeward of Custom House wharf, went astern against Merritt's Wharf, and will [have] doubtless received considerable damage as the tide falls.

The Schooner "Lily" of Carlton, [operated by] Captain Turner, had to leave Reed's Point wharf, about 9:00, in tow of the tug Relief. She had a collision with a ship lying at the end of Gerow's Wharf and carried away her flying jib-boom and two starboard stunchions [actually stanchions, which are posts or supports]. During the collision, [one] of the hands called "Ben," belonging up the river somewhere, was missed, and not having returned to the vessel for an hour after she was safely made fast at Gerow's Dock, it is feared he was drowned. The Empress wharf is a complete wreck and the warehouse is broken in two. There is not a wharf in the City that has not suffered more or less damage, and many of them are complete wrecks. Charlotte and Water Street Extensions were both submerged and much of each has been washed away. Most of the lower floors of the warehouses and stores on the South Market Wharf are flooded, and proprietors were busy hoisting their goods to the floors above. a schooner laden with iron is said to have been sunk at Sand Point. a large fence in Smyth Street in front of the vacant lot owned by Mr. Dunlap is blown flat to the ground. The damage down around the harbour is almost unprecedented, and we fear there will be a sad record of loss, both of life and property, when all is known.

The Tide was at its height at 9:00, and when the turn came it subsided very rapidly. The wind began to go down at the same with time, and before midnight was comparatively calm. a dense fog set in, and the sound of the fog whistle was heard during the remainder of the night.

At the Marsh Bridge and all round Courtney Bay, the water was very high, covering the bridge to a depth of 18 inches [45 centimetres] *and making passing inconvenient. Fences were blown down in that direction and in other parts of the City.*

The Chimney of the Revere House, and other chimneys were blown down; also a cooper's shop in Water Street and several old houses.

Two houses at the head of Reed's Point wharf were vacated by their inmates last evening, the wharf having begun to fall in around them.

– *The St. John* Daily Telegraph, *Tuesday, October 5, 1869*

Raging Storms of the 1870s

1870 to 1873
The Atlantic Region

THE PREDICTION OF WEATHER has never been an exact science. Even with all of today's modern technology, there always remains a degree of chance that a storm could cause unforeseen havoc across a given region. An unexpected change in track. A system stalling. An unusual tide. A passing cold front. A rise in water temperature. Any of these factors could cause a forecast to prove faulty and affect the course of history for positive or for negative.

Whereas today we have the luxury of satellite and radar images to aid our meteorologists in the prognostication of weather phenomenon, such was not the case in the 19th century. Weather reports of even the most severe storm were relayed from person to person, community to community, and often, when the grey clouds descended, few people realized the extent of the wrath that Mother Nature was about to exert. The history of Atlantic Canada is littered with examples of catastrophic storms that left a swath of death and destruction in their wake.

Such was the case during the early 1870s, an atypically turbulent decade in the weather history of Eastern Canada. Each year, around the beginning of June, as the waters along our Atlantic Coast began to warm, men and women alike knew that for the next six months, coastal regions would be susceptible to the hurricane menace. Be it a Cape Verde–born system that began off the coast of Africa and slowly climbed its way across the Atlantic, gaining strength as it moved, or a storm born in the western half of the Atlantic when a tropical depression encountered unexpected sources of strength, only to turn and churn to the north, there were always storms to fear.

The 1870s began on an innocuously quiet note. After the first several months of the 1870 Atlantic hurricane season passed without incident, the calm of late summer quickly turned to destruction.

The only storm of note that year occurred in the late evening of September 3, the centre passing close to Nova Scotia's coastline. But it was enough to make locals take notice. Mather DesBrisay, a judge and historian in the village of Bridgewater on Nova Scotia's LaHave River, recorded in his *History of the County of Lunenburg* that:

> *"In the early morning hours of Sunday, September 4th, a great gale blew across Nova Scotia, caused by the storm passing parallel to the coastline on the province's south side. Trees were rooted out in all directions throughout Lunenburg County and, in Bridgewater, the frame for a new rectory being built in the community was blown down."*

Meanwhile, in the neighbouring community of Mahone Bay, the frame of a new schoolhouse under construction in the port community was blown clear over, and other buildings along the province's southern shoreline were tossed and levelled into the surging Atlantic brine. Many fishing vessels also bore the brunt of the storm and, according to DesBrisay, the vessel *Onward*, which had been driven ashore near the village of Chester, lost four of her crew as a result of the early September storm.

In 1871, three major storms systems passed through the Maritimes in a span of six weeks, between August 30 and October 13, on their way to death in the icy waters south of Greenland.

The storm that passed through the region in the overnight of October 12 was one that stood out in the memory of Judge DesBrisay on the South Shore of Nova Scotia.
On that Thursday, around mid-afternoon, a wind began to
pick up in the coastal fishing community of Lunenburg.
Blowing out of the east, the gusts steadily increased until
after the supper hour, when the wind suddenly began
coming hard in from the south—a sure sign that a major
northbound storm was about to descend upon the region.
Beginning its extratropical transition (changing from
a tropical cyclone to a temperate system), the storm came
ashore north of Halifax, along Nova Scotia's Eastern
Shore, and cut a swath across the province, through Pictou
County, before exiting near Prince Edward Island and
into the Gulf of St. Lawrence.

On the South Shore of Nova Scotia, DesBrisay recalled
that the storm blew a "perfect hurricane," battering the
region with more rain and wind than it had witnessed in
years. Matters were compounded by an unusually large
storm surge that hammered away at wharves and fishing
boats in coastal centres, including Lunenburg. One
captain, William Young, tried in vain to save his vessel,
the *Busy*, but he had to seek refuge in a sugar barrel as the
incoming tide rolled over him, sweeping him along for
several blocks.

The year 1872, one of the calmest on record in the
Atlantic, saw the formation of only five storms, none of
which achieved the wind-speed equivalent of today's
major Category 3 storms. One system, having under-
gone extratropical transition, skirted the coast of Nova
Scotia on the night of October 28. Two other systems
affected the waters off Newfoundland's south coast in
September.

As trying as the first three years of the 1870s had been
for storm-savvy residents in northeastern North America,

nothing could quite prepare the residents of Nova Scotia and Newfoundland for what was to come in 1873. That year proved to be one to remember in what would become Atlantic Canada. Although only one major system tracked through the region during the June and November hurricane season, it was one that would go down in not only regional but also international lore.

The storm became popularly known as the Great Nova Scotia Cyclone, or the Nova Scotia Hurricane of 1873, depending on which circle you were in, in the era before hurricanes were given friendly names. The second major storm centre to form during the 1873 hurricane season, it was eventually ranked by the National Hurricane Centre as the 53rd deadliest hurricane recorded between the years 1492 and 1996.

Sadly for Atlantic Canada, much of the calamity associated with the destruction probably could have been avoided, because many areas were amply warned about the impending storm. This storm was the occasion of the first hurricane warning, when the United States Army Signal Corps warned of the storm approaching the coast between Cape May, New Jersey, and New London, Connecticut. The storm didn't make landfall anywhere near those areas, however. And, ironically, thanks to a failure of the telegraph line to Halifax, people in Ontario knew more about the approaching storm than did most in the Atlantic region. Weather bulletins had been relayed to Toronto from Washington, D.C., warning about the track of the hurricane ascending the Atlantic shore, but those bulletins never made it to Halifax.

Like most weather systems that wreak havoc in the North Atlantic, the storm of 1873 was a Cape Verde–type storm that formed off the west coast of Africa and gained strength as it crossed the Atlantic in tropical waters. It became a hurricane on August 17 and appeared to be on a collision course with the United States East Coast before assuming a slow northeasterly track as it passed west of Bermuda. It gained strength to Category 3 and ultimately passed just to the east of Nova Scotia as a Category 2 storm before finally making landfall by careening into the Avalon Peninsula area of Newfoundland.

The highest sustained winds in this storm were recorded at 185 kilometres per hour. It's likely that a particularly warm Gulf Stream helped the hurricane to maintain its strength that year. On August 24 it passed by Nova Scotia en route to Newfoundland, where it roared over St. John's. According to Environment Canada (EC), estimates of casualties range from 500 to 600. Other reports suggest that the death toll was possibly as high as 1000 in all of Atlantic Canada. The damage totalled an estimated $3.5 million, which converts to approximately $69 million in 2007 dollars. a total of 1200 vessels and 900 buildings were reported destroyed. Intense thunderstorms and rainfall in excess of 50 millimetres were reported in Halifax, Truro and Sydney. According to EC, the weather observer working in Sydney stated that the storm was the worst to pass over the region since 1810.

One positive thing to come out of the storm, again according to EC, was that the telegraph failure caused an uproar and inspired politicians to put a better storm warning system in place, but it would be years before the Atlantic region would be ravaged by a hurricane of such proportions again.

David Phillips is a senior climatologist with 38 years' experience with Environment Canada as of this writing. He says that contrary to popular modern belief, not all storms are disastrous to the Atlantic Canada region.

"In a way," he explains, "hurricanes are a good news story, although we often only hear about the negatives, which can be substantial depending upon the severity of the storm."

Although it is common to think of the destruction, and sometimes death, that can be associated with these storms, as Phillips also points out:

> *"The rains fill the reservoirs and rivers, and replenish the moisture in the soil. We don't think of that. We tend to think about property being lost and trees coming down and all the destruction, but that's only natural. These are serious issues, to be sure, and I wouldn't want to diminish* [the acknowledgement of] *those impacts in any way, but hurricanes often get an unfair treatment in the sense that there is some value to them. If you did a cost analysis, I would guess that it would end up being more positive than negative, particularly in the Maritimes."*

Typically, Phillips says, the Maritime region tends to get the rain but not necessarily the strong winds. "Of course, there are all kinds of exceptions that we can find if we look back over the history of the region."

In the late 1990s and in the early part of the new century, the number and severity of hurricanes seem to have increased, but Phillips says it is difficult to identify any specific pattern, because many things influence a hurricane, particularly in the colder waters of the North Atlantic. "For instance, a storm hitting Florida will often bring heavy rains, strong winds, severe thunderstorms and imbedded tornadoes that cause millions of dollars worth of damages and, ultimately, death. But when that same storm pushes through the Maritimes, we usually get the welcoming rains that end the drought, that douse the forest fires, that bring welcome relief, but we seldom get the strong winds," Phillips observes.

Of course, that doesn't hold true for every storm, but he says:

> *"Even when the more powerful storms do hit the region, they are not as severe as those down south. That's because when they arrive here, they're moving a lot faster than when they were in the southern hemisphere. In the lower latitudes they tend to stall out over a region, and they batter the area for an extended period. That's why they can cause so much damage. But in the Atlantic region, they don't stand around and clobber you like they do in the warmer climate. When they come to the northern waters, they're usually spent out and they're anxious to die. They're best described as hit-and-run storms in Canada. They're forced along by the cooler temperatures, and that's a good thing."*

Phillips describes hurricanes as the "greatest storms on earth." As he elaborates, "They pack the greatest wallop, they are what we consider the monster storm. They are huge in a geographical sense, as they can reach over 1000 kilometres. Some of them are larger, some smaller. Some are wound up pretty tight, while some are spread out over a large area. And most hurricanes pack a powerful punch when they're at their peak."

All hurricanes, even those monster storms that kill and cause millions of dollars worth of damage, start the same way, Phillips explains. Hurricanes usually form 10 to 20 degrees north of the equator. "They all start as your everyday garden variety thunderstorms that coalesce and come together, drawing energy and moisture from the warm surface of the water." That's why, potentially, there could be hundreds of them in any given season.

They begin as tropical depressions, which are clusters of thunderstorms with winds at up to 62 kilometres per hour, often in the Gulf of Mexico or southern Caribbean, but many begin off the coast of Africa. "As they move across the Atlantic," Phillips observes, "they pick up more heat and energy from the ocean. In order for those storms to form a hurricane, the temperature of the ocean must be at least 27°[C] or warmer. Anything less would not sustain the storm. We get what we call a tropical storm when winds reach 63 kilometres per hour, and that basically means the storm is becoming more organized, that the thunderstorms are getting stronger, and we begin to see the formation of the eye."

When hurricanes hit the colder Canadian waters, they lose intensity, because they lose their fuel of warm water. "But very few make it. Many, many things influence the formation of a hurricane—water temperature, water depth, favourable winds, air pressure patterns. Any one of these factors can bring down a storm, and it will fizzle out. That's what happens to most of them," he explains. "On average, only about seven of these storms make it to hurricane status in any year." But there are exceptions. In 2005, for example, there were 28 named tropical storms.

To be considered a hurricane, a storm must pack winds higher than 118 kilometres per hour, and that force must be sustained for at least an hour. That would make it a Category 1 on the Saffir-Simpson Scale. Storms with sustained winds of 154 kilometres per hour are considered as Category 2 hurricanes. To be classified as Category 3, storms must have sustained winds of 178 kilometres per hour, whereas Category 4 storms pack winds of 210 kilometres per hour. a Category 5 storm would have winds of at least 250 kilometres per hour.

Phillips says that Category 1, 2 and 3 storms can be destructive, but Category 4 and 5 storms can be catastrophic.

Fortunately, Atlantic Canada has never been hit by a Category 5 storm. "Only about 7 percent of the storms that enter Canadian waters would have a chance of being greater than a Category 3," he adds.

These days, Phillips says, unlike in the past, meteorologists are fairly accurate when it comes to forecasting storms, usually giving people in the projected storm track time to prepare:

> *"A hundred years ago or fifty years ago, we didn't have the ability to pinpoint a system, so the only way you knew a storm was coming was when it sank a ship or made landfall. By then, it was too late. It was already upon you. Most times today we can pinpoint the track and even predict its intensity before it hits. Of course, all of that can change, but the science is improving."*

Based on past historical data, it is easy to see why people fear hurricanes, and Phillips says he understands that anxiety. "They can be deadly and destructive," he says. "We've seen that over and over throughout our history. However, even with past tragedies, I always say that I've never met a natural disaster that couldn't be worse than it was."

Hurricane Juan & White Juan

September 26, 2003, and February 17, 2004
The Maritime Provinces

THE LATE 20TH AND EARLY 21ST CENTURIES have brought strange and often dangerous weather phenomena to seemingly all parts of the globe. Floods in China, severe cold in Europe, drought in Africa and a host of other extreme conditions have put the entire world on edge. Notice has been served, it seems, that we, as humans, are having a significant ecological impact on the environment around us and that the global climate is currently undergoing a massive change for which we are very much responsible. Even the most ardent of skeptics now seem willing to admit, after years of research, that something is wrong with our weather patterns and that global warming, brought about by human action, may be the culprit. And, while the past decade has seen severe weather grip other parts of the world with increasing frequency, we here in Atlantic Canada have been far from immune.

During the decade leading up to Hurricane Juan in 2003, 1995 brought an especially tumultuous Atlantic hurricane season. With a total of 19 named storms, from Allison to Tanya, it still ranks as one of the busiest seasons on record. The front that would develop into Hurricane Luis began brewing in the western Atlantic on August 27. Over the course of the next 16 days, it would gather up steam in the Atlantic, all the while beginning a slow climb into the Gulf Stream, bound for Eastern Canada. The Maritime provinces managed to escape its wrath, but Luis was far less kind to Newfoundland. Crossing the southeastern part of the province on September 10 and 11, it dropped as much as 127 millimetres of rain in the process. Fierce wind gusts topped out at 130 kilometres per hour.

According to the Canadian Hurricane Centre, the Cape Verdi–type storm, which was still of hurricane force when it hit Newfoundland, generated waves as high as 30 metres, as observed from the luxury liner *Queen Elizabeth II*, which was caught on the periphery of the storm. Fortunately, damage to the province was light, with only one fatality directly linked to the storm. Elsewhere, Luis' toll had been much worse. In the Leeward Islands, 16 people were killed when the storm hit, and it caused billions of dollars in structural damage. As a result of the 1995 storm, the name Luis was retired from the list of hurricane monikers.

With only thirteen named storms, six of them major, the 1996 hurricane season was a respite compared to the previous year. Although somewhat quieter, the season still produced its fair share of demon storms that brought torrential rain and some destruction to Atlantic Canada. Hurricane Hortense was one such storm, although initially it appeared as if it wouldn't pose much of a threat. After meandering across the Atlantic, beginning on September 3, she reached the Caribbean on September 7 and only then gained tropical storm status. But, from there, it was a quick jump to becoming a major hurricane. Hortense passed through the Turks and Caicos and across the Dominican Republic, gaining strength all the while. It briefly attained Category 4, with winds exceeding 200 kilometres per hour, on September 13.

By the time Hortense began to travel north towards Canadian waters, the storm had lost some steam. But, even still, Hortense hit southern Nova Scotia on September 15 as a Category 1 storm—the first storm this intense to make landfall in Nova Scotia since Blanche had hit the region more than two decades earlier. The power outages and damage to both human-built and natural structures, caused by 120-kilometre-per-hour winds, amounted to roughly $3 million in Nova Scotia. The next spring, because of the damage this storm had wrought along western Atlantic shores, the name Hortense was officially retired from the list.

After a few years of relative calm in the Atlantic, the silence was broken by Hurricane Gustav in September 2002. After forming as a tropical storm on September 8, Gustav was given hurricane status just before noon on September 11. At the time, the storm was south of the Maritimes and represented a clear and immediate danger to the region. According to Environment Canada, the storm tracked over land on Cape Breton Island, approaching from the south, near St. Esprit Island, a little more than 13 hours later. Rain doused the province, with most areas receiving at least 50 millimetres and some regions receiving as much as 102 millimetres, with wind gusts as high as 122 kilometres per hour reported at Cape Sable in the province's south. Gustav also produced intense storm surges throughout the Maritimes, but especially along the shores of Prince Edward Island, where the high tide made for dangerous circumstances. A total of 4000 people lost power, and, although the winds sent many tree limbs flying and there were multiple reports of localized flooding, there were no fatalities.

As intense as the three preceding storms had been, nothing could have prepared the people of the Maritimes and, in particular, the people of Nova Scotia, for the storm that would descend upon them in late September 2003. Formed near Bermuda, the storm that would become known as Hurricane Juan began accumulating strength in the warm waters of the Atlantic's Gulf Stream, reaching hurricane status on September 26. The next day, Juan had escalated to a Category 2 storm and reached peak intensity, with winds around 160 kilometres per hour.

In September 2003, Canada's Maritime provinces were walloped by Hurricane Juan, one of the most power hurricanes to ever hit the region. Coastal infrastructure and forests suffered the most damage.

~•∞ৎ•~

After moving slowly towards the north and west, on September 28, Juan took an abrupt turn to the north and increased in speed. Because of its rapid movement, Juan had little time to lose intensity over the increasingly cold waters of the Atlantic as it continued on a collision course for Nova Scotia. The following day, Juan made landfall near Halifax, at this point only slightly less intense than at its peak. Massive storm surges in excess of 2 metres were reported in Halifax Harbour. To the south of the city, a newly installed boardwalk along Hirtle's Beach near Lunenburg was tossed aside by the wind like a leaf on the breeze. In Green Bay, a seaside community on Nova Scotia's South Shore, pieces of pavement were literally ripped free of the ground and tossed onto the lawns of cottage owners.

The storm passed across the province, affecting many towns, including Truro, before hitting Prince Edward Island as a tropical storm. Some residents of Prince Edward Island and Nova Scotia were without power for more than two weeks after the event, with hundreds of thousands of people left in the dark in the hours during and immediately following the storm. Environment Canada estimated that as many as 100 million trees were lost throughout the Maritimes because of the storm. Halifax's Point Pleasant Park was especially hard hit, with over 90 percent of its mature growth damaged or destroyed by the force of the winds. Because of the level of damage and the unexpected deaths (a total of six—two directly from the storm, four others from indirect causes), the name Juan was retired from the list of storn names in the spring of 2004.

News reports from throughout the region related the story of Hurricane Juan. The *Bulletin* in Bridgewater, Nova Scotia, ran the following story a few days after the monster storm rocked Atlantic Canada:

> "*Hurricane Juan smashed into Nova Scotia with destructive force late Sunday night, causing widespread power outages, snapping trees like dry twigs and battering coastlines.*
>
> "*The Category 1 storm hit the Halifax Regional Municipality the hardest, but the fury of in excess of 120 kilometres per hour winds and storm surges were felt along the South Shore as well. Green Bay, Cherry Hill, Mahone Bay, Crescent Beach, Fox Point, Chester and Blue Rocks were among the most affected. Part of the Point Road in Blue Rocks was decimated to rubble.*
>
> "*Crews were out clearing trees, limbs and seaweed from roads throughout Lunenburg County, sometimes*

with snowplows, in the night and well into the morning. Paul Sampson, an operations coordinator for the Transportation and Public Works Department, was out Monday assessing the status of the Green Bay Road.

"'There was considerable damage to the road, a lot of the chip seal has been removed, and a lot of the armour rock has been misplaced...the road has been removed right up to the asphalt," he told reporter Keith Corcoran. "We've got the road open now if anybody needs to get through for an emergency.'

"Marguerite Isaacs, a resident of Green Bay in Lunenburg County on Nova Scotia's South Shore, told Corcoran that Hurricane Juan was worse than her experience with Hortense, which hit Nova Scotia in 1996. "'We lost our van in Hurricane Hortense, but this one is worse...talk about powerful, it ripped up the pavement and put it on our lawn.'"

"On Hermans Island, another small South Shore hamlet, David Smith came within a whisker of becoming a casualty of the storm. He and his wife were watching television at their cottage during the height of the hurricane when a 12-metre spruce tree snapped and crashed onto his verandah.

"'I was very lucky," he told Corcoran. 'Another couple of feet and it would have come through the window right where I was sitting.' Although the Smiths were fortunate the tree narrowly missed the main section of the building, it did wipe out a section of glass railing on the deck which had recently been installed."

"There were two confirmed casualties in the Halifax area as of Monday. Two people died when trees fell on their vehicles. One was a paramedic who was killed when a tree crashed into an ambulance."

Afterwards…

The traumatic experience that Hurricane Juan brought to the residents of Nova Scotia in the fall of 2003 was enough to make them aware of the awesome power of extreme weather. It was, by all accounts, the single worst storm to make landfall in the region in more than 100 years. And, as many have said since then, Juan surely is one of the signs that some global environmental disturbance is afoot. But, although signs of climate change are most commonly associated with wet, warm and wild hurricanes, extreme weather of other forms can also suggest climate change.

Such was the case, just five months after Hurricane Juan, when a winter storm, dubbed "White Juan" by the media, rolled through the Maritimes. A classic nor'easter, the storm formed on February 17. It developed intensely and accelerated as it moved over the water up the Atlantic Coast. On February 19, it began snowing in Nova Scotia, and, soon afterwards, it was snowing in all three Maritime provinces. With high storm surges reported in many areas, wind gusts in excess of 120 kilometres per hour and lightning pockets embedded within the blizzard, the storm was for all intents and purposes the wintertime equivalent of a hurricane. A total of 95.5 centimetres of snow fell at Canadian Forces Base Shearwater, smashing a record set 40 years earlier by more than 20 centimetres. Similar new milestones were notched throughout the region, from Yarmouth to Charlottetown.

Dubbed "White Juan" by the media, the blizzard virtually shut down the entire region for several days. Believe it or not, this is a row of vehicles.

One of the interesting aspects of the storm was the compact swath of snowfall. Although Moncton, New Brunswick, received in excess of 60 centimetres of the white stuff, roads in Fredericton, just over an hour away by car, received only a fine dusting. In the aftermath of the storm, thousands were left without power, and the copious amounts of snow proved difficult to dispense with, especially in metropolitan areas, where major arteries, normally four lanes across, were reduced to one passable pathway. Many schools in Nova Scotia were closed for as much as a week because of the wintry blast. White Juan truly was a reminder that the wrath of Mother Nature can take on many varied and destructive forms.

In September 2003, when Nova Scotians hunkered down in their homes as Hurricane Juan battered the province, we thought the day of reckoning had come at last. With predictions of doom ringing in the air and dire warnings that "the big one" was about to hit, we prayed the storm would spare us its fury.

There were tense hours leading up to Juan's arrival and then watching in utter disbelief and horror as one of nature's most powerful forces attacked everything in its path, leaving a swath of destruction that is still being cleaned up today in 2007. Nothing was spared. Entire forests were toppled. Buildings were reduced to piles of rubble and splinters. Boats were tossed around in the bays and harbours like toys in a bathtub. Service infrastructure was rendered useless. People were killed. Entire communities were left in darkness for days, even weeks. Juan's legacy, including millions of dollars of damage, was a grim reminder that we cannot escape the wrath of Mother Nature.

In the wake of Hurricane Juan, people were plunged into new lows of despair. Such a terrible disaster just doesn't happen here, or so we naïvely believed. We were wrong, and we received a rude awakening. However, in the larger scheme of things, we now know that the situation could have been much worse. Two years later, Nova Scotians and the rest of the world watched in utter disbelief and shock as hundreds of thousands of Americans in the southern states of Louisiana, Alabama, Mississippi and Georgia struggled to survive in the terrible aftermath of Hurricane Katrina. In what was surely the worst natural disaster in the history of the United States, if not North America, the toll exacted by Katrina leaves one awestruck. The sheer magnitude of the death and destruction throughout the four Gulf Coast states was difficult to fathom. Hundreds died from the hurricane itself and the resulting floods in New Orleans, and tens of thousands of

Americans were left homeless, refugees in their own, rich country. As for economics, the storm's financial cost soared into the billions. It will take years for communities to rebuild and citizens to reestablish their lives, if they ever can following such a disaster.

Atlantic Canadians have known tragedy throughout our history, but nothing on the scale of Hurricane Katrina. By comparison, Hurricane Juan was but a gentle breeze and the rains nothing more than a light shower, but it was still a force that shook up this province. Imagine the fury of a storm five times worse than Juan. It's a frightening prospect, but it's one that we must think about. With God's grace, we can hope never to know such force, but we must not be so complacent as to think we are immune to such a disaster. Hurricane Juan and the several blizzards that struck this region the following two winters serve as reminders to Atlantic Canadians that we must be forever mindful that no place on earth is immune to nature's fury.

Sinking of the *Titanic*
The Halifax Connection

April 14, 1912
The North Atlantic, 1300 km east of Halifax, Nova Scotia

> *"I will say that I cannot imagine any condition which could cause a ship to founder. I cannot conceive of any vital disaster happening to this vessel. Modern ship-building has gone beyond that."*
>
> *—Edward J. Smith, Captain of RMS* Titanic

ON THE NIGHT OF APRIL 14, 1912, three operators—Walter Gray, Jack Goodwin and Robert Hunston—had taken up their positions at the Marconi wireless telegraph station at Cape Race, a point of fog-shrouded, flat, barren land located at the southeastern tip of Newfoundland's Avalon Peninsula. The Cape Race station, built in 1904, was the first wireless station in Newfoundland. It would be one of two land-based locations that received the distress call from the RMS *Titanic,* the other being the Marconi telegraph station on top of Wanamaker's department store in New York City.

There had been reports throughout the day of icebergs being spotted in the north Atlantic shipping lanes. Ships, including the RMS *Baltic,* which was operated by the same company as the *Titanic,* had been sending out warnings advising of large ice floes in the region. It was at Cape Race that the first hint of any problem with the *Titanic* was heard.

The *Titanic* was about 650 kilometres east of Cape Race when the three men stationed there noted indications of impending disaster. Robert Hunston immediately began the message log copied below. Note that the *Titanic*'s shipboard time was one hour and 50 minutes ahead of Eastern Standard Time, which was used at Cape Race, and that the initial distress call was the old CQD, which stands for "Come Quick Distress"; it had officially been replaced in 1906 by SOS (contrary to popular belief, SOS is not short for any particular phrase but was simply an easy message to send and recognize in Morse code).

April 14th

- 10:25 PM (EST) [12:15 AM on *Titanic*]
  J.C.R. Goodwin on watch hears Titanic *calling C.Q.D. giving position 41.44 N, 50.24 W about 380 miles* [610 kilometres] *SSE of Cape Race*

- 10:35 PM
  Titanic *gives corrected position as 41.46 N, 50.14 W. a matter of 5 or six miles* [8 or 10 kilometres] *difference. He says "have struck iceberg".*

- 10:40 PM
  Titanic *calls* Carpathia *and says "We require immediate assistance." Gray on duty.*

- 10:43 PM
  Titanic *gives same information to* Californian, *giving* Titanic's *position*

- 10:45 PM
  Caronia *circulates same information broadcast to* Baltic *and all ships who can hear him. RH on duty.*

- 10:55 PM
  Titanic *tells German steamer "Have struck iceberg and sinking"*

- 11:00 PM
Titanic *continues calling for assistance and giving position*

- 11:25 PM
Establish communication with Virginian *here and give him all information re:* Titanic, *telling him to inform captain immediately. OK.*

- 11:36 PM
Olympic *asks* Titanic *which way latter steering.* Titanic *replies "We are putting women off in boats"*

- 11:55 PM
Virginian *says he is now going to assistance* Titanic. Titanic *meanwhile continues circulating position calling for help. He says weather is calm and clear.*

April 15th

- 12:50 AM
Virginian *says last he heard of* Titanic *was at 12:27 AM when latter's signals were blurred and ended abruptly. From now on boats working amongst themselves relative to* Titanic *disaster. Nothing more heard from* Titanic.

- 2:05 AM
First message from New York asking for details. This is followed by about 300 more, chiefly from newspapers to many ships asking for news.

- After Daylight
News commences to arrive from ships stating Carpathia *picked up 20 boats of people. No word of any more being saved.*

End

The RMS *Titanic* was owned by the White Star Line. An "Olympic Class" vessel, she sank on her maiden voyage in the North Atlantic, sending a stark reminder of humanity's limits against the fierce forces of nature.

The *Titanic* was built in Belfast, Ireland, at the Harland and Wolff Shipyard. The ship was heralded as White Star's masterpiece, the latest triumph in its ongoing battle with the rival Cunard Line. At 269 metres in length and having a "gross register tonnage" (internal volume) of 131,108 cubic metres, the *Titanic* was unlike anything else on earth, outclassing every vessel that had come before her. The majestic luxury liner had seven decks that provided every convenience her passengers might desire. Those amenities included a state-of-the-art gymnasium, a swimming pool, a Turkish sauna, three elevators, a post office and, for first-class passengers, a lavish dining room and richly appointed cabins.

On her maiden voyage, which began on April 10, 1912, in Southampton, England, the *Titanic* was bound for New York City. On board were many of the era's rich and famous personalities. The ship's manifest reveals that there were a total of 2224 people, including 899 crew members, on board. Among the most prominent passengers sailing on the voyage were railroad magnates George Widener and John Thayer; multi-millionaire John Jacob Astor and his wife, Lady Astor; well-known mystery writer Jacques Futrelle; fashion designer Lady Duff-Gordon; millionaire director of Quaker Oats, Walter Douglas; well-known theatre producer Henry Harris; and United States President Taft's military aide, Major Archibald Butt.

The record shows that the *Titanic* ran into an iceberg while travelling south of the Grand Bank, about 640 kilometres south of Newfoundland, on Sunday, April 14, 1912, thereby causing catastrophic damage. After listing for about two hours and 40 minutes, the "unsinkable"

On its maiden voyage, the *Titanic* hit an iceberg about 640 kilometres off the southern coast of Newfoundland. Just two hours and 40 minutes later, the "unsinkable" luxury liner vanished into the cold, murky waters of the North Atlantic.

super ship disappeared into the cold, inscrutable brine of
the North Atlantic, just before 2:30 AM on April 15. The
exact number of people who perished when the *Titanic*
sank has been debated over the years. British officials
reported a loss of 1490. However, a subsequent American
investigation later pegged the number at 1522. Either
way, it was a tragedy.

The *Titanic* met its fate at 11:40 PM. Frederick Fleet and
Reginald Lee were the two lookouts stationed in one of
three crow's nests high above the ship's deck. They had
been stationed there to spot for icebergs; they should have
had binoculars, but these essential aids had apparently
been taken away by a ship's officer. Unfortunately, as
a result, their warning came too late; the ship was almost
on top of the darkened iceberg before the alarm rang out.
With a tremendous impact, the floating mass of ice
slammed into the starboard (right) side of the ship, rip-
ping open five of the *Titanic's* watertight compartments
below the waterline. One pump managed to keep ahead
of the incoming flow of water for a time, but it was a perilous situation. The *Titanic* had been designed to stay
afloat with as many as four of her compartments flooded,
but five was too many, and the massive vessel began to
list. Captain Edward Smith sent out a team of inspectors.
When they informed him that the ship was in trouble, he
ordered that lifeboats be readied by about 12:30 AM, some
45 minutes after the impact. Unfortunately for those on
board the listing luxury liner, there was only room for
fewer than half the passengers in the lifeboats. Most of
the people on board were already destined to die that
fateful night, and the predicament was worsened by passenger skepticism regarding the seriousness of the situation, so many lifeboats left only partially full.

In the aftermath of the *Titanic* disaster, Halifax, Nova
Scotia, would play a prominent role in what had become

A major cause of the loss of life was the insufficient number of lifeboats the *Titanic* had on board. These were some of the lifeboats that carried some of the survivors.

~∽◯C∾

the first true international media event of the 20th century. Richard MacMichael is the coordinator of visitor services and a senior interpreter at the Maritime Museum of the Atlantic in Halifax. He is considered to be an authority on the *Titanic* disaster:

> *"We see that almost immediately in the hours following the collision, that word arrives in Halifax, and the news spread quickly, as one would expect with a tragedy of such importance. This was a huge story of international proportions. The next morning in local papers and even in the New York Times, you get stories proclaiming that* Titanic *had hit an iceberg and has sunk.*

*It was an unthinkable but fascinating story, unlike
anything we had seen before. In keeping with the
urgency, we also see that there were some wildly conflicting reports of loss of life, particularly that* Carpathia *had rescued everyone on board, which of course
we know today just wasn't true.* Carpathia *had rescued only 705 survivors. There were also conflicting
reports as to where* Carpathia *was heading. Initially, it
was reported that she was coming into Halifax with her
survivors, and that immediately put the city on the
radar as people boarded trains for Nova Scotia. Then*
Carpathia *changed course and goes into New York
City, so when people arrived here expecting to find survivors, they were greatly disappointed."*

In the hours following the sinking, the White Star
Line began its cleanup and public relations operations.
MacMichael notes that Halifax was the closest mainland
port of call to the disaster site, so company officials
quickly arrived in the city, and Halifax was immediately
thrust into the limelight as it became the focal point for
search and rescue operations. "It would have been
quicker to send vessels out from Newfoundland to the
site where *Titanic* went down, but then any bodies
retrieved would have had to have been put on another
boat and sent back to the mainland, so why not just use
Halifax in the first place, since there were train lines for
the immediate transportation of bodies. That was their
thinking."

Initially, two Halifax-based vessels were dispatched to
participate in the retrieval of frigid corpses from the
ocean waters. The *Mackay-Bennett* and the *Minia,* a pair of
telegraph cable–laying ships, were hired by the White
Star Line to participate in the recovery efforts. The vessels, each with a crew of between 15 and 20 men, had on
board a member of the clergy to perform burials at sea
and an undertaker, and the recovery ships' supplies

included 100 coffins, canvas body bags and tonnes of ice to preserve the human remains.

The *Mackay-Bennett*, with Anglican minister Rev. K.C. Hind aboard, left port on April 17 and arrived at the *Titanic*'s last reported location on April 20. The *Minia*, with Rev. Henry W. Cunningham of St. George's Anglican Church in Halifax, left port on April 22. In total, the *Mackay-Bennett*, which became known as the "death ship," retrieved 306 bodies during her initial search, but many were in such bad shape that they could not be identified or embalmed. As a result, 116 people were given burials at sea. The remainder were placed in the ship's hold and on the deck for transport back to Halifax. When the *Mackay-Bennett* entered Halifax Harbour with its morbid cargo, the entire city stood still as tolling church bells told the mournful news of its arrival.

The second cable ship, the *Minia*, recovered 17 bodies. The *Montmagny*, a Canadian government lighthouse supply ship, with Rev. Samuel Prince of St. Paul's in Halifax on board, found four bodies in early May. Hired in mid-May to do another sweep of the area, the Newfoundland sealing vessel *Algerine* recovered only one victim of the *Titanic* tragedy, that being steward James McGrady. Then, about a month after the sinking, the transatlantic liner *Oceanic* came across a lifeboat with three more corpses, but no other bodies were recovered.

In Halifax, the return of the human remains presented local authorities with a host of problems and challenges, MacMichael explains:

> *"They had this issue of how to deal with the bodies. They knew they would have people coming into the city to retrieve loved ones, but the question was, how to identify so many bodies, particularly when many remains had no immediate identification on them. John Henry Barnstead, the deputy registrar of deaths for*

Nova Scotia at the time, came up with a detailed system
of listing all personal effects and all details about the
body, no matter how insignificant it seemed, because it
may actually lead to one of the bodies being identified.
Years later in 1917, his system was used again to iden-
tify victims of the Halifax Explosion."

Some bodies were easily identified, but others were
impossible to name:

"They had bodies of people who had been in a hurry
to leave the sinking ship, and they didn't have one piece
of identification on them. About half were fairly easily
identified, [John Jacob] Astor of course being among
them. Some members of the crew, like steward Herbert
Cave, were also easily identified because among his per-
sonal affects was a copy of the first class passenger list
with names checked off of the people whose cabins were
his responsibility. Like any good dutiful employee, he
wanted to familiarize himself with his charges to add
a bit of a personal touch, and hopefully that might lead
to a nice little gratuity."

As the bodies were brought in on the cable ships—the
remains of the prominent passengers in coffins and those of
crew and third-class passengers wrapped in canvas—they
were all taken to a temporary morgue that had been set
up in the Mayflower Curling Rink on Halifax's Agricola
Street. With its sheets of ice, the curling rink, as the largest refrigerated spot in the city, was the best choice for
laying out the bodies until they could be dealt with.
Undertakers John Snow and Company oversaw the handling of the victims with the assistance of 40 additional
embalmers who came from throughout the Maritimes to
help. (Five years later, the rink building would be completely knocked down by the Halifax Explosion of 1917,
but that's another story.)

In total, 209 bodies were returned to Halifax, with only 59 of them being forwarded to family for their burial. Eventually , the remains of 150 *Titanic* victims were buried in three Halifax cemeteries.

~~○※○~~

MacMichael goes on to discuss how the crew members of the ships dispatched for cleanup duty were affected. "The effect on the crew members on board the two cable ships often goes unmentioned, but we know it was significant. Their job was to go out to retrieve, repair and replace damaged sections of transatlantic cable, and, if they weren't doing that, they were laying new cable. There was nothing in their job descriptions about fishing the frozen bodies of men, women and children out of the North Atlantic. We can assume these crews saw some disturbing images, and that must have been difficult for them. Things like that cannot be easy to forget," he explains.

In describing what they found when they arrived in the North Atlantic at the site where *Titanic* went down, one crew member on board the *Mackay-Bennett* is quoted as once saying, "As far as the eye could see, the ocean was strewn with wreckage and debris, with bodies bobbing up and down in the cold sea."

The clergy members on board these vessels performed burials at sea, MacMichael tells us, but they also undertook to provide moral and spiritual support for the crews. As a show of gratitude for his support, the crew of the *Minia* presented Rev. Cunningham with what is today considered the star artifact in the Maritime Museum of the Atlantic's permanent *Titanic* exhibit. "The crew had recovered one of *Titanic*'s deck chairs, and they presented it to Rev. Cunningham as a way of saying thanks for his assistance. One of Rev. Cunningham's grandsons later passed it on to the museum."

As well, the *Minia* crew had also recovered the body of a young boy whose identity remained a mystery. He became known as the Unknown Child, and MacMichael says the boy's recovery hit the crew hard. "His death really took hold of these men's hearts, so much so that they bought the little white coffin for him to be buried in and they paid for the memorial stone for his grave."

In total, 209 bodies were returned to Halifax, with only 59 of them being forwarded to their families for burial. Between May 3 and June 12, 150 bodies were eventually buried in three Halifax cemeteries: 121 bodies in the nondenominational cemetery at Fairview Lawn, 10 in the Baron de Hirsch Jewish Cemetery and 19 in the Mount Olivet Catholic Cemetery. MacMichael explains, "The reason some identified bodies were buried in Halifax is because their families could not afford to bring their loved ones home. This was particularly true for third class passengers and members of the crew. They just did not have the money, so their family member ended up being buried in Halifax."

It is interesting to note that one of the graves at the Mount Olivet Catholic Cemetery is that of J.F.P. Clarke, the bass player in the ship's band, which, according to legend, played "Nearer My God to Thee" as the *Titanic* sank into the cold Atlantic that fateful night in April.

Also of note is the grave of James Dawson in the Fairview Lawn Cemetery. Dawson was a "trimmer" in the engine room—his job was to lug coal from the bunker area to the boilers. It would have been one of the lowest paying jobs on the ship. Because his grave marker reads just "J. Dawson," many people think it is the final resting place of Jack Dawson, a fictional character played by Leonardo DiCaprio in James Cameron's 1997 blockbuster movie, *Titanic*, the all-time top money-maker in cinematic history. Again, the success of that film proves that the sinking of the *Titanic* has left an insatiable appetite for this legendary story, which has become ingrained in our collective psyche.

It is not well known that two *Titanic* passengers had connections to the city of Halifax. One was Hilda Mary Slayter, who was travelling back to Canada for her wedding. She survived the disaster and subsequently married the wealthy British Columbian man she was sailing to meet when she nearly went to her death along with so many other *Titanic* passengers. Years later, she returned to Nova Scotia, where she lived until her death. She is buried in Halifax.

George Wright, a prominent Halifax personality and millionaire, was not as fortunate as Miss Slayter. He perished in the icy Atlantic Ocean along with the hundreds of other *Titanic* victims.

In the aftermath of the *Titanic* sinking, new safety regulations were put in place. North Atlantic steamships were immediately fitted with additional lifeboats, and, in time, international regulations would dictate the number of lifeboats required in relation to the number of passengers. Additionally, mandatory regular safety drills were instituted on board all vessels.

In 1985, a team of French and American researchers discovered the *Titanic* wreck site about 3.8 kilometres below the surface of the Atlantic. Today, the fatal voyage of the *Titanic* is part of our culture, immortalized forever in movies, songs and books. Jack Thayer, son of *Titanic* victim John B. Thayer, is quoted as once saying, "The 20th century began the night the *Titanic* sank."

Profound words, indeed. The *Titanic* catastrophe was the first time in modern history that so many people of prominence were laid low at the same time. Following the sinking of the luxury liner, in quick succession, the world saw the outbreak of World War I, the stock market crash, the Great Depression, the eruption of World War II—and society has been barrelling full steam ahead ever since.

Although the *Titanic* sinking is arguably the most famous Maritime tragedy, there have been many others, among them the Canadian Pacific's *Empress of Ireland*.

On her first trip, during the summer of 1914, the *Empress of Ireland* sailed away from her berth in Québec Harbour bound for Liverpool, England. Fate, however, had disaster in store for the *Empress of Ireland*. Only hours into her voyage, she collided with the Norwegian collier (coal ship) *Storstad* in a sudden fog and sank in the Gulf of St. Lawrence. The *Empress of Ireland* took all but 462 of the 1477 souls to the bottom with her.

Some four decades before the *Empress of Ireland* and *Titanic* tragedies, the RMS *Atlantic* sank, with the loss of 546 lives. Like the *Titanic*, this luxury steamship was built by Harland and Wolff in Belfast, Ireland, the second ship to be built by this yard in a special agreement with the recently reorganized White Star Line. Constructed in 1870, when transatlantic steamers were just starting to hit their stride, she was fitted with both a 600 horse-power (447 kilowatt) steam engine to power her single propeller and four masts that could be outfitted with sails. On June 8, 1871, she commenced her scheduled service between Liverpool, England, and New York City.

In the case of the *Atlantic*, it was voyage 19, which began in Liverpool on March 20, 1873, that would prove deadly. Believing that heavy seas earlier in the trip had left the coal supplies lower than expected, Captain James Williams decided to detour to Halifax, Nova Scotia, to replenish them. Despite little local knowledge and a storm that brought heavy seas and reduced visibility, the captain maintained a speed of 15 to 22 kilometres per hour as he headed the ship for Terence Bay, Nova Scotia. Little did he know as he left the bridge at midnight that the *Atlantic* was dangerously off course to the west.

In the wee hours of the morning of April Fool's Day, 1873, with the fourth officer at the helm, the *Atlantic* struck an underwater rock off Mars Head, near the town of Lower Prospect, Nova Scotia. As the ship began to take on water and sink, the crew sprang into action to launch the lifeboats, but all the port (left) ones were quickly swept away by the waves, and the starboard (right) ones were rendered unusable by the ship's list. Many people were washed off the deck into the roiling water, but ropes heroically run to shore allowed some people to be saved, and local fishing boats rescued others. The final death toll was given in a government report as 545 out of a total of 957 passengers and crew (although another source says

Great August Gales

August 1926 and August 1927
Near Sable Island in the Atlantic Ocean

As THE SUN ROSE ON THE MORNING of Saturday, August 7, 1926, out in the middle of the Atlantic Ocean, an eerie calm hung in the air like the hushed silence of a morgue. A dense, thick fog embraced the vessels anchored on the rich fishing grounds, wrapping them in a lingering cool moistness that permeated the fishermen's heavy clothing. It was quiet and still, except for the light waves lapping against the hulls of the boats, licking them with their salty kisses. There was no wind. Fog is usually the order of the day at this location, so there was no indication of anything unusual in the weather. All appeared to be in order.

A dozen fishing boats were anchored off Sable Island, the only visible part of a huge conglomerate of shoals and sandbars that cover some 25,000 square kilometres. Known as the "Graveyard of the Atlantic" because of the shipping hazards, the waters around the island have been a favoured fishing ground for centuries. The fishing was still good in the early 1900s, with plenty of haddock, hake, pollock, halibut and cod. Vessels would stay for several days until their holds were full before heading back to Nova Scotian home ports such as Lunenburg, Liverpool, Cape Sable and Yarmouth, where they'd unload the catch and prepare for the next trip. Among the schooners stationed near Sable Island on this particular day were the *Annie Conrad, Silver Thread, Golden West Two, Mary Ruth, Sylvia Mosher, Sadie A. Knickle* and the famous *Bluenose*.

Days start early for the fishing fleet. On this morning, the men arose at 4:00. After a hearty breakfast, they lowered away the dories, one man in each, and prepared for the long hours of fishing that followed. The day was uneventful, as fishing days go. By nightfall, however, these same vessels would be fighting for their very existence, battling against hurricane-force winds and tremendous seas, with waves so big they could swamp a fishing boat with one try. The vessels fishing close inshore on the windward side of the island would have little chance. The wind would rise and strike with such deadly speed that by the time the men were back on board, dories hoisted into their moorings, fish dressed and the hatches battened down, it would be too late to hoist sail and head for safety. Vessels anchored on the north side, in the lee of the island, would be more fortunate, and most would escape with just minor damage.

Back in 1926, few ships had wireless equipment, and little means of communication with the mainland existed. To compound matters, there were no reliable weather forecasts. Instead, skippers had to rely on barometer observations coupled with their own judgement and years of experience to warn them of approaching storms. However, this particular August gale came with none of the usual indications of a hurricane. When it struck, it would do so with a sudden and violent fury that even the fastest schooners of the day would be unable to outrun.

In good weather, the shoal waters around Sable Island were a treacherous enough place for ships. In bad weather, the seas became seriously perilous. Even a moderate increase in wind could turn an easy swell into a short, powerful, breaking sea capable of imposing terrific strains on an anchored vessel and causing many to run aground. A schooner caught on the windward side of the island in a big blow had either to attempt to race off to the lee shore with the help of engines, if she had any, or sail along the shore until clear of the bars.

The morning had seemed like any other morning out on the Atlantic Ocean. The water had been calm, with hardly a ripple. The relative stillness had allowed the men in the dories to load the fish onto their schooners with ease. Suddenly, as if out of nowhere, tiny puffs of wind blew toward the island, a sign that a storm might be brewing. At around 2:00 that afternoon, several schooners fired their "swivels" (small cannons) to signal the men in the dories to quickly return to their vessels. Because their day was only half done, the dorymen knew that something must be wrong. This warning was only used in the face of impending danger, so they understood that they should not delay.

With the men back on board, the fish were quickly dressed and stowed in the hold, every last piece of equipment secured and every hatch locked down. Without communication from the mainland, the fishermen had no way of knowing what type of storm was heading their way. As the winds gained momentum, though, it became clear that a serious storm was coming, and the seasoned captains realized that there was no way to outrun it. By 9:00 that night, the seas near Sable Island had become a furious place, with walls of water the size of mountains. Waves crashed over the schooners, throwing gear overboard and threatening the lives of every crew member.

Aboard the *Bluenose*, the "Queen of the North Atlantic," the crew was bracing for the worst as the swells tossed the schooner about as if it was a toy in a bathtub. Positioned at a place known as the "Bend" near Sable Island, the *Bluenose* raced for her life. Built for speed, the sleek, streamlined vessel rode the crests with impressive agility.

At age 15, Clem Hiltz was the youngest and least experienced crew member on the *Bluenose*. He was terrified. He feared they had little hope of ever returning to Lunenburg in the face of such a powerful storm—the kind from which tragedies are born—as did the other 26 men aboard the schooner, with one important exception. The storm would not triumph if Captain Angus Walters had anything to say about it.

"What are we going to do?" the inexperienced young seaman asked the seasoned captain. "The seas are fierce and there doesn't look like any end in sight. We're taking on water... The waves must be 60 to 70 feet [about 20 metres]."

"Head to the hold," the veteran sea captain commanded his crew. His reputation for getting the *Bluenose* out of tight spots was legendary. "Remain there 'til she blows over."

Lashing himself to the wheel, Captain Walters became one with his vessel. Riding the mountainous waves with the skills of an experienced seaman with many years to his credit, he was not ready to let his ship go down without a fight.

Captain Walters remained at his station for the next eight hours, eventually manoeuvring the schooner over the sandbar at Sable Island to deeper water and, finally, to safety.

Two other vessels—the *Sylvia Mosher* and the *Sadie A. Knickle*—were not as fortunate. They were lost, along with all crew members. The *Mosher* was carrying a crew of 25, and the *Knickle* had a contingent of 24 men. The first "August Gale" had struck with deadly fury.

According to the old United States Department of Commerce Weather Bureau, the storm appears to have been the second hurricane of the 1926 Atlantic hurricane season.

It originated in the open mid-Atlantic east of the Lesser Antilles and approached North America in a clockwise curvature, forming around August 1. It attained Category 3 strength off Bermuda. By the time it reached the waters off Nova Scotia, sometime between August 7 and 8, the storm underwent extratropical transition near Sable Island.

Vivian Corkum of New Cumberland (a small hamlet located near the town of Lunenburg) was just five years old when her father, Walter Wamback, was lost with the schooner *Sadie A. Knickle* in the August Gale of 1926. Still, she retained vivid memories of the event, which also claimed the vessel *Sylvia Mosher*. "The night of the storm I remember waking up and seeing my mother at the window...and I remember her saying, 'I hope Papa doesn't get drowned tonight,'" Mrs. Corkum once recalled in an interview with the *Lunenburg Progress-Enterprise*. "She was very worried, but then so were all the women."

Having headed out to sea in June, the vessels were finishing up their major summer trip on the notoriously treacherous but lucrative fishing grounds off Sable Island when the storm struck. August was known to be a time of bad weather on the Atlantic, but the fishing was so good in that area that staying through the month was seen as a calculated risk. Unfortunately, being weighed down with fish would work against the vessels. Also, although people ashore knew the storm was coming, they had no means by which to inform the vessel crews. Fishing schooners did not carry radio receivers in those days, so it would be late August, even September, before many of the sailors' families would learn the fate of their loved ones.

There is a well-known story in the town of Lunenburg of one little girl who would walk to the local store every day to see if there was any word yet of her father. Eventually, after more than two weeks, it was learned that the girl's father was one of those lost at sea.

Mrs. Corkum remembered that she was back in school by the time her family found out the terrible news about her father's boat. "I don't know if someone actually said it to me or if I just sort of absorbed it," she recalled in the interview. "A Captain Parks (the vessel's part owner) had been there. I guess he brought the news."

At such a tender age, Mrs. Corkum doubted she really understood the significance of what she was hearing. "I just knew that my father wasn't coming back, but it seemed to me that he would come back, because he always did."

An uncle, William Wamback of Broad Cove, and two distant cousins, the brothers Parker and Wade Wamback, who, like her father were from Mount Pleasant, were also lost. "Almost the whole community was in mourning," said Mrs. Corkum. Even the families who had not lost loved ones were suffering over the tragedy, "because they realized it could easily have been them."

In late September, a memorial service was held for the lost crews, and Mrs. Corkum remembered how strange it seemed at the time. "There were so many people that they brought the organ out on the step and held the service outdoors. It was the first time I'd been to an outdoor church service." She could still remember her puzzlement over the thick, black armband worn by the captain's son. "I didn't know what it was for."

The community of Blue Rocks, another small settlement on the outskirts of Lunenburg, was one of those areas struck hard by the gale of 1926. There was hardly a house or home, certainly not a family, that was not immediately affected by the terrible storm. In several cases, fathers, sons and brothers had all been lost with a single ship.

But this tragic tale of death and loss on the high seas does not end here—this is only the beginning.

On August 24, 1927, just a few weeks past the first anniversary of the first storm, a second gale hit with a force that surpassed even the first. The second August gale took four schooners to the bottom of the Atlantic. The American schooner *Columbia*, a racing rival of the *Bluenose*, was also lost, along with her mostly Nova Scotian crew, and many other mariners narrowly escaped death. Also lost in the 1927 storm were the *Uda R. Corkum*, with 21 men; the *Joyce Smith*, with 22 crew members; the *Clayton Walters*, with 21 casualties; and the *Mahala*, which had 20 people on board. Counting deaths on both land and at sea, a total of 184 people perished in Nova Scotia during the 1927 storm, and 80 of the dead were fishermen from Lunenburg.

The 1927 storm had formed in the open Atlantic east of the Lesser Antilles on August 19 and reached Nova Scotia while undergoing extratropical transition on August 24, hitting Newfoundland by August 25. Like the storm in 1926, it is likely, based upon the track, that it was a Cape Verde–type storm that gained strength as it headed across the Atlantic. The storm track took it directly over Yarmouth County. It was the first major storm of the 1927 Atlantic hurricane season, reaching Category 3 status at its height, but it had diminished in strength by the time it made landfall over Nova Scotia. Nevertheless, the winds were in excess of 160 kilometres per hour. Nova Scotia received more than 100 millimetres of rain, undoubtedly adding to the calamity.

There was sufficient warning for shipping ahead of this storm, because hurricane notices were issued for New York northwards as early as August 21. However, because fishing boats were not yet equipped with radio receivers, this news had not reached the captains and crews already at sea.

Lack of communication with the ships at sea was also a problem in assessing the impact of hurricanes. Family members had to rely on reports from other vessels that may have spotted the whereabouts of the schooners upon which their loved ones served. What's worse, according to the Nova Scotia Museum, is that after such severe storms, little wreckage typically washed ashore, making it even more difficult to determine if a vessel had been lost or if it had simply found shelter against the storm in another port and would thus be taking its sweet time to get home. Initially, as many as 75 boats were considered missing as a result of the 1927 storm. An example of the degree of loss felt by single families was the *Mahala*. Warren Knickle, its captain, was lost, along with his brothers, Owen and Granville, and brother-in-law Scott Miller. The impact of losing four bread-winning males must have been devastating for the extended Knickle family. Many Nova Scotia families affected by the storm received financial compensation for the loss of their loved ones, but money could not replace a life.

Both the ferocious August 1926 storm and its twin in 1927 caused all manner of mayhem, including the loss of six local schooners with 138 men on board. Together, these two powerful storms were responsible for the highest non-war-related death toll in the history of Lunenburg County, Nova Scotia.

Ralph Getson, curator at the Fisheries Museum of the Atlantic in Lunenburg, has devoted many hours to researching and talking about the Great August Gales of 1926 and 1927. He says that although other storms have hit the Nova Scotia fishing fleet, nothing can compare to these two gales for the utter destruction and loss of human life they left in their wake.

"In the Maritimes, we know that we get tropical storms that come up the eastern coast every year, and the people of this region have learned to accept that and to cope," Getspn explains. "But nothing could prepare anyone for the extent and amount of devastation, and it was made worse because, while the people on shore knew the storms were coming and they could take precautions, the men on those fishing schooners were like sitting ducks on a pond. They were at the mercy of Mother Nature, and she wasn't very forgiving on these two dates."

Men who take to the seas in the once-lucrative fishing industry know and understand the dangers. They respect the sea and the challenges it can sometimes throw at them. However, when hit by a storm of such magnitude, Getson notes that there isn't much anyone can do—except pray.

"When a storm comes up while you're out there on the open sea, the captain knows his only hope of survival is to get away from the islands. Those sand bars [of Sable Island] go out some 22 miles [35 kilometres] under the water from the land mass. In the midst of such a storm, there was no way these vessels could get away from the islands. They would have been pretty heavy with months' worth of catch in their holds. It's likely they hit the land mass, broke up and sank," he says. "In fact, the ships basically disintegrated. They didn't find much of the schooners. They did find the water tank and a barrel head from the *Sadie A. Knickle*, but that's it. Sometime later, part of a railing believed to be from the *Sylvia Mosher* was recovered, but that's basically all there was. There weren't any other signs of these schooners, which tells you just how powerful this storm was."

Eventually, one body was recovered from the lost crews, Getson relates. The remains of Thomas Martell from St. Peter's, Cape Breton, the cook on board the *Sadie A. Knickle*, came ashore on Sable Island, but his body was in such bad shape that his daughter had just his clothing and tattoos by which to identify him. He was buried on the island.

"That was just one example of how truly devastating these storms were," Getson emphasizes. "They wiped out entire families, and the impact was felt all over the province, but mostly here on the South Shore [of Nova Scotia]. The *Sylvia Mosher* was out of Lunenburg and the *Sadie A. Knickle* came out of LaHave River [near Bridge-water]. When you had a chance to go out on a boat, you took it—and if there was an opening for another person, you usually spoke for a family member. That's how it worked. The storms took fathers, sons, brothers, brothers-in-law—it didn't matter. When these vessels went down, these men didn't stand a chance."

Fishing is a dangerous way of life, and the families in Atlantic Canada have learned to deal with tragedies. But none like this. However, even after the storm of 1926, the men knew they had to go again the next season. "They just had to," Getson explains. "There wasn't any choice. No matter how much you grieved for the other guy and his family, when it was time to go to sea, you went. You just think it will never happen again. Besides, what's the chances of two major storms hitting two years in a row? After the first one, they just considered it a one-off. It was an act of nature—a brutal act of nature, mind you—but nonetheless, you just didn't think these types of tragedies are going to happen back-to-back. They faced the ocean and away they went... Only, we now know there was a second storm, and it was worse than the first."

Although little changed in the year between these two storms, Getson observes that a great deal changed after the storm of 1927. "In 1928, for example, they started putting radio receivers on board all vessels, so the captains could at least get news from the shore, especially the weather reports. That way, at least they could have some advanced warning if a storm was heading their way. Ship-to-shore [two-way] radio didn't come around until the 1930s, and it wasn't until 1933 that the first Lunenburg-based fishing schooner had a ship-to-shore radio."

As well, following the double tragedy, the fishing companies issued a directive that there could be no more than one member from a family on board a vessel at any given time. "That way, an entire family wasn't wiped out if a vessel should happen to go down. Doubling up [of family members on the same boat] still went on, but nothing to the extent that happened before these storms. The companies really discouraged it, and we know now that was a good thing," Getson continues.

Additionally, the companies started to fit their vessels with engines, so they didn't have to rely on sails in the midst of such conditions. "That really was the beginning of the end for the days of vessels being powered solely by sails," concludes Getson.

There is an old saying among seafarers that goes like this: "Red sky at night, sailors delight. Red sky in the morning, sailors take warning." If only the crews on board these ill-fated schooners had received some warning, who knows how many lives might have been saved? This question can never be answered, but Getson prays—and believes—that scenarios like those of 1926 and 1927 will never be repeated.

Newfoundland Tsunami

Tsunami—a Japanese word meaning "harbour wave"

> *"Suddenly without warning, there is a roar of waters. Louder than that of the ordinary waves on the shore, it breaks on their ears, and then, with a shuddering crash, a 15-foot* [4.5-metre] *wall of water beats on their frail dwelling, pouring in through door and window and carrying back in its undertow, home and mother and children!"*
>
> —The November 22, 1929 editorial
> in the *St. John's Daily News*

THE BURIN PENINSULA REGION of Newfoundland was first given the name *Buria* by Basque fishermen centuries ago. *Buria* is an old Russian word that carries the meaning "tempest," so it should come as no surprise that this small swath of land off the south coast of Newfoundland is known for its stormy weather and rough conditions. But what washed ashore on November 18, 1929, was no storm. No, it was a force of nature much more powerful. At that time, keep in mind, Newfoundland was not yet part of Canada but was instead a self-governing dominion.

The product of undersea volcanic eruptions, landslides, certain kinds of earthquakes or a combination thereof, tsunamis are massive, fast-moving waves that rush outwards from an epicentre, wreaking havoc on whatever land they encounter. Tsunamis are generally associated with the Pacific Ocean, so any occurring in the Atlantic Ocean would be considered unusual, indeed.

But, just after 5:00 PM on November 18, 1929, a powerful earthquake occurred on the Grand Bank, a major fishing ground off Newfoundland's coast that fuelled the province's economy. The resulting disturbance, which included a major underwater landslide, registered a score of 7.2 on the Richter scale; it was strong enough to be noticed in Montréal and New York City. Transatlantic telegraph cables were damaged, and regular shipping traffic was disrupted. The tsunami was so powerful that the remnants of it were observed in places as distant as South Carolina and Portugal. The earthquake's epicentre was at 44.69 degrees north and 56.00 degrees west, about 250 kilometres away from the nearest land—Newfoundland's Burin Peninsula.

The three tsunami waves produced by the underwater disturbance came ashore along the Burin Peninsula around 7:30 PM and left a swath of destruction unlike anything previously recorded here. According to the Library and Archives of Canada, the waves travelled at a speed in excess of 129 kilometres per hour. More than 40 tiny hamlets and coastal fishing communities, accessible only by ship, were swamped by the waves. It took three days for emergency supplies to begin arriving in the region, and relief efforts were hampered by a blizzard that struck the day after the waves. The loss of property because of the tsunami eventually came in at a total of over $1 million, a substantial figure in those days and equivalent to $12 million in 2007 dollars. Over 10,000 people were left homeless. The tsunami resulted in 27 immediate deaths (and one delayed one) on the Burin Peninsula; one additional casualty occurred on Cape Breton, where the force of the wave was also felt in certain coastal areas.

Years later, E.P. Reddy, the former mayor of Marystown, a community on the Burin Peninsula, recalled that the ordeal was as frightening as one could ever imagine. In February 1978, Reddy recounted as part of a Heritage Week speech how Marystown had experienced its share of serious sea tragedies:

> "...the schooner Orion in November 1908, after the season voyage loaded with heavy salted codfish, left a port on the Labrador for Marystown via Grand Bank. She was lost with all on board; eight married men from Marystown; three men from Grand Bank; one from Fortune; one from Brunette, leaving many widows and orphans.

> "Then again, the August Gale of 1936, when a tornado blew in from the sea, striking the headlands of Cape St. Mary's, where a large number of our little fishing boats were fishing at the time. The storm came so unexpected and the winds were of such velocity, it took our fishermen unaware as it smashed their boats to pieces against the jagged rocks of that rugged coast. There was no escape. Some 25 men, again from Marystown South, lost their lives. I was the wireless operator, and for days I did nothing but copy telegrams conveying the tragic news. These tragedies are felt to this very day...

> "On November 18, 1929, about 7:00, an earthquake and tidal wave struck Marystown as well as the whole Burin Peninsula. I was postmaster and assistant wireless operator at the time. I was sitting at the wireless desk when the earthquake struck. The whole office building shivered and stuttered like a frightened steed. The wireless set went dead immediately, and we were isolated from the outside world for four days. I left the office immediately for my home in my own little rowboat across the harbour. I could barely pull with all my might against the rushing tide, which I could not understand,

as I never experienced such tide before. I just reached the South Side, however, when the water began to come back. A wall of water about 10 feet [3 metres] high came rushing in, sweeping wharves, [fish] flakes and stores all before it until it spent itself across the Garnish Road into the Southwest Marshes."

Historian and retired schoolteacher Robert Parsons, who wrote about the stories of Newfoundland in his book *Born Down by the Water,* has researched the deadly tsunami that hit his home province in 1929, and he says the destruction from the massive waves was far-reaching and absolute, destroying just about everything that stood in the water's path.

"People had no way of knowing what was coming until it hit them," Parsons says. But he quickly adds, "Even if they had known what was about to happen, what could they have done? The people had not heard of such a thing before. They didn't know what a tidal wave was or what it could do. In all likelihood, they would not have known what to do."

What could they have done? Where could they have gone? Where could they have hidden? What precautions could they have taken?

"There is an interesting story—perhaps only local folklore—but it tells of a Frenchman who had been living in one of the villages when the people felt the earth shake. The story goes that this Frenchman, who had heard about tidal waves, bent down and put his ear to the ground. He then predicted that the region was going to be hit by a tidal wave. Apparently, nobody paid him any attention. But what would they have done? There was nothing to do, as they didn't know if this supposed wave was going to hit in an hour, 10 hours, or 10 days.

They were at the mercy of nature that day, and nature wasn't feeling particularly forgiving."

Parsons says this disaster hit these communities hard. The victims were modest people living off the land and the sea. They didn't have much. Even their homes were modest. When these massive walls of water hit their villages, the buildings buckled under the mighty force.

Although the immediate monetary loss and human suffering caused by the tsunami was eventually tabulated, Parsons observes that the long-term effects of the enormous tidal wave were felt for decades. "These people were survivors, they knew how to rebuild their communities, but what they couldn't do was control the natural repercussions."

For instance, he explains, the natural disaster had destroyed the fertility of the Grand Bank fishing grounds. "There was very little fish left on the Burin Peninsula for about 10 years after the tidal wave. Why? Because for six or seven years after the tidal wave, there was no squid, and as squid was the bait fish for cod, it meant if there was no squid, then there was no cod. Plain and simple. And if people couldn't fish, they couldn't survive. It's something that often goes overlooked when people are discussing the tsunami, but this was the beginning of the Great Depression, and people had it hard. The collapse of the fishery left these communities with little hopes of recovery from such a disaster."

The people of Newfoundland are resilient, and, as the years wore on, Parsons says, they managed to rebound and rebuild their lives. And although one might expect that the residents of the Burin Peninsula would live in fear that another tsunami could hit the area, he says that isn't the case. The deadly tsunami that hit southern Asia on December 26, 2004, reminded Newfoundlanders of this painful chapter in their own history, but they did not dwell on it. They know that these disasters can happen, but they refuse to let fear dominate their lives.

On January 23, 2007, citing recent tsunamis in Southeast Asia, the Honourable Stockwell Day, Minister of Public Safety, announced that the federal government was initiating an Atlantic tsunami warning system. Although the Pacific Ocean, where over 70 percent of tsunamis have historically occurred, already had a tsunami warning system, no such system previously existed for Canada's Atlantic Coast and the Gulf of St. Lawrence. The Department of Fisheries and Oceans is the agency primarily responsible for the new system. The federal departments of Natural Resources, Environment Canada, and Public Safety and Emergency Preparedness, provincial emergency management agencies and the United States National Oceanographic and Atmospheric Administration are also involved in the project.

Equipment and procedures already in use to predict storm surges, which are much more frequent occurrences in the Atlantic region, will be enhanced for this purpose, with the additional benefit that storm-surge prediction will also be improved. Day observed that quakes, whether on land or under the sea, and their effects can have a dramatic impact on coastal communities, and that the new system will allow the authorities to quickly alert eastern Canadians of possible danger.

As the Honourable John Baird, the current minister of the environment, explained, "By linking with the existing weather warning system through Environment Canada's Atlantic Storm Prediction Centre, the new tsunami warning capability ensures Canadians will have access to timely early warnings which may someday save many lives."

For a setup cost of approximately $250,000 and an additional $125,000 per year, the government expects to be able to issue tsunami alerts within 10 to 20 minutes of an Atlantic-region quake when appropriate. Mariners and coastal dwellers both stand to benefit from the new system. With this kind of advance warning, we can only hope that Eastern Canadians will be able to escape in time to avoid any future events like the Newfoundland Tsunami of 1929.

Escuminac Salmon Disaster

June 19 and 20, 1959
Escuminac, New Brunswick

TODAY, ESCUMINAC, NEW BRUNSWICK, has a population of less than 250. The community is located in Northumberland County, along the entrance to Miramichi Bay. According to historical data, the community was originally founded by Irish and English settlers, but the widespread French presence in northeastern New Brunswick has changed the ethnic composition over the years. But fishing has long been, and remains, the village's heartbeat.

Garth Williston had just turned 19 years of age in April 1959, and, like most other young men from Escuminac, he had been fishing for several years by that time. He had been helping on the boat operated by Wendall Williston, his father's cousin. In those days, salmon and mackerel were the catches of choice, and this season the word around Escuminac was that the salmon run was strong, with large catches. There had been reports of some boats returning to the wharf with upwards of 100 salmon per trip and, at $5 per fish, that translated into a lot of money in 1959 (equivalent to $36 per fish in 2007 dollars).

"We had heard that there was a big run," Garth recalls. "And if you had a chance to go after that kind of money, you took it, but I can say without question that if anyone in the fleet thought for one second that there was any kind of danger, they never would have gone out that night. There's no way they would put their lives on the line like that. These captains had been on the seas all their lives. They knew when it was safe to go out but in this case, there just wasn't any warning."

Escuminac was the gathering point for small fishing boats averaging between 10 and 12 metres in length. The Escuminac salmon fleet in those days consisted of about 50 vessels. Each boat was equipped with a "back sail" to balance the effect of the main sail, thereby allowing the ship to remain pretty well motionless without any work on behalf of the crew while "drifting" for salmon. On most days, the salmon fishermen left port between 4:30 and 7:00 PM and set their nets at depths of about 24 metres in the Northumberland Strait and Miramichi Bay. Then they would drift all night while the salmon got caught in their nets. The next morning, between 6:30 and 10:00, they returned to port with their catches. Crews usually consisted of a captain and one or two helpers. Rarely, four men were on board.

Traditionally, the salmon drifting season started around June 1 and lasted for about three weeks while the fish were running. Despite a downturn during the early 1950s, by 1959 the catch was on the rebound. An average night's work usually saw the boats bringing in around 50 salmon per trip.

Garth recalls that on this particular night, a Friday, the weather was not good. "In fact, it had been a pretty bad week, and I remember a lot of the boats stayed in because it was so cold and damp," he says as he relates the conditions of June 19, 1959. "It was dreary and over-cast, with northeast winds blowing pretty much all week. And it was cold, too. It may have been the middle of June, but we were dressed for winter weather. I had on my winter coat and underwear and a winter shirt. It was colder than normal, and I remember it pretty well. I know I had a sore throat that day, and I blamed that on the weather."

Maybe it was a sign, he reflects, but, based on long-range forecasts, there was no indication that the weather was going to get any worse. "If there had been any hint of how bad things were going to become, the boats would never have left the wharf, I can tell you that much for sure. These were seasoned captains with lots of years of experience. No matter how well the salmon may have been running, they never would have taken a chance... No way."

With every expectation of a successful night, Garth and Wendall got their gear and stores ready and loaded them onto the boat. They left the Escuminac wharf sometime around 4:00 that afternoon, but not before checking the forecast one more time.

"That was always the last thing any good captain did before leaving the wharf," he points out. "And it didn't sound bad to us. It didn't sound like anything to worry about."

Weather reports suggested that the wind was going to blow out of the east at 24 kilometres per hour and then change over to northeast, blowing at 32.

"It didn't sound bad," Garth says. "Most captains figured that wind wasn't enough to hurt anyone. We left the wharf, and we were among the third bunch of boats to go out."

He recalls that after leaving the wharf, they ran northeast of the Escuminac breakwater for maybe an hour. "There, we set our nets, put the sail up; and the boat began to drift back with the wind. It was blowing a breeze at that point, but we thought it really wasn't anything to worry about. It wasn't anything that we couldn't handle. We had seen these conditions before."

After setting the nets and completing their chores, Garth says they caught a few cod, had some supper and then went to sleep. On the boats, he explains, it is important to catch some rest whenever possible because during a normal trip the men can expect to be up several times throughout the night.

"This night didn't start out too bad," he says. "He [Wendall] didn't get much sleep, but I did manage to doze off a few times."

Trying to sleep on board a fishing boat is a unique experience, Garth points out. "Just when you'd nod off, the seas would wake you. Sometimes the big waves would smash up against the side, and the boat would jump and splash around. That can be pretty unnerving at times, especially when the sea is big. And then sometimes just the loud roaring of the seas can wake you up. It was pretty loud that night."

Somehow, Garth managed to get a few hours of rest that night, but he had no idea what was going on around him out on the water.

By the time he got up the next morning, at around daybreak, the fog had closed in around the boat. "It was a really messy, dirty day, and, to make matters worse, we didn't know exactly where we were, as the high seas had pushed us further than we had thought. But wherever we were, we knew we didn't want to be there, because—in this heavy sea—we wanted to be out in deep water. We could hear the breakers, and we could tell that we had drifted too close to the shoals, and that wasn't good in this fog. Then we saw the light at the Escuminac east breakwater, and we knew we had to get out of there before we ran aground."

The Escuminac east breakwater is the easternmost point of New Brunswick, and Garth remarks that in bad weather it was not the place any boat wanted to be. If they had grounded in such high seas, Garth notes, there was no telling what would have happened to them. "But it wouldn't have been good, let's just say that."

Just when Garth and Wendall began preparations to head for open water, their nets became entangled in some lobster gear they had not seen, and, to make matters worse, the foot line of their net became wrapped in the lead line, so that it became more like a huge, heavy cable. "Imagine what that thing was like, trying to pull it in," Garth recounts. "It was pretty heavy, and then, as we thought we were making headway, the sail mast snapped off in a big gust. Then, all of a sudden, the boat went up in a big sea, and she came back down, fast and heavy. We didn't get the nets in fast enough, and they got caught in the rudder. We worked for a while, and somehow we managed to get it clear. We then hauled the nets in as fast as we could because we knew we had to get out of there."

Minutes later, the boat was hit by another large wave. "That one swept the nets back overboard, and this time it took me with it," Garth recalls:

> "I really have no specific recollection of anything before hitting the water. The first thing I remember was being in the water, and it was cold. When I came up, I was bobbing in the high waves looking back at the boat and he [Wendall] was pointing for me to grab the net so that he could pull me in. Somehow, I managed to reach out and grab hold, and—let me tell you—no one could have gotten me to let go. Let's just say I was hanging on for dear life. When he got me and the nets to the boat, he reached down and pulled me in with such force that I lost one of my rubber boots, but that was the least of my worries."

Once Garth was back on board, Wendall grabbed an axe and cut the net loose. He knew it was the only way to get the boat clear of the lines that threatened to entangle their rudder and propeller. With the rudder and propeller tangled, they would have been trapped there, danger-ously close to the shoals.

"Now free of the nets, we hightailed it out of there and headed to deeper water, where we thought it would be safer," Garth continues. "By this time, there still wasn't much rain, but it was fogged in pretty thick, and the wind was blowing well over 100 miles an hour [160 kilometres per hour]. We could see other boats that were a lot worse off than us, but we had problems of our own, so we couldn't help them much. To keep from being swamped, we had to man the pumps, but soon we were on open sea, and we had deeper water under us."

Just as the two fishermen thought they had made a successful escape, their boat quickly turned sideways against the big sea, and the water hit the starboard (right) side, forcing the boat to go up while the port (left) side went down. "It was like we were up in the air, practically upside down. I remember looking down and thinking it was like there was nothing under us holding up the boat. As the breaker poured in the high side at the back, I just thought, that was it. I thought there is no way we're getting out of this," Garth admits. "But somehow the boat righted herself, and down she came with a thud. And the water rushed in with such force that it would have taken us over the side if we hadn't braced ourselves. We had taken on a lot of water, but somehow we were still afloat and still in one piece. We pumped her out again and then we were on our way."

Steering towards the shore, Garth says it wasn't long before they could see the breakwater at the Escuminac wharf, and they knew that although they were close, they still weren't out of danger. Following a series of manoeuvres through the breakers, the two were finally able to tie up at the wharf. It was now about 8:30 in the morning, several hours after their struggle for survival had begun, just around daybreak. They had been through quite an ordeal, but miraculously they had made it back alive, and the boat was still in one piece. Many others, however, were not so fortunate.

As the other boats in the fleet slowly began arriving back at the wharf, Garth says it became painfully obvious just how tragic this storm had been. "We had no idea. We had no radio when we were out there, so we didn't know what the other boats were up against, but it wasn't good."

He recalls one boat drifting back in past the breakwater at around 11:00 that morning. "It wasn't a pretty picture. Half of the bow was out of it, and the captain was jammed back under the other half. He was dead. And the young fellow that had been on board with him was in the water. a rope was over the end of the bow and was wrapped around the young fellow's ankle. He must have gotten tangled up in it somehow. He was dead too."

It was a tragedy for the entire community, Garth recounts:

> "A lot of boats drifted back in, and they were in similar condition. They'd come in, some would be empty, some would have bodies on them, and some boats were never found."

He admits that being one of the survivors can carry a tremendous amount of guilt with it. "The way I figure it, is that you can't be held accountable for that. Basically, I say you have to have some luck some time, and that was a good time to have it. I think I was young enough that it really didn't bother me, but I know the disaster ruined the lives of a lot of people," Garth admits.

However, he adds, two days after that storm, most of the surviving fleet was out at it again. And Garth was right there with them.

❦

The storm that hit the salmon fishing fleet on the night of June 19 and 20, 1959, claimed the lives of 35 fishermen from Escuminac and the surrounding area and sank 22 vessels from the region.

According to records, it was no run-of-the-mill squall that blew up and ran ashore that night and caused so much trouble. The waters in the St. Lawrence around this part of New Brunswick can be treacherous, but the disaster was caused by a storm system that blew in on a northeasterly track. It had begun a few days earlier, when a tropical depression passed over Florida, bringing heavy rains to that state, before progressing into the Atlantic. Once on the open ocean, the system intensified and developed first into a tropical storm, then into a hurricane, as it tracked northeast midway between the North American mainland and Bermuda. By the time the storm reached the Maritimes, it had become an extratropical depression. It passed close to much of the Nova Scotia coast then took an abrupt turn towards land near Cape Breton Island. The storm entered the Northumberland Strait, (which lies along the coasts of Prince Edward Island, Nova Scotia and New Brunswick) and eventually backtracked its course and went out to sea after a duration of roughly 12 hours. Winds peaked at about 130 kilometres per hour.

At the time, the storm system was not named, because it was not believed that it had reached hurricane strength while in the Atlantic. Subsequent analysis suggested, however, that the storm had indeed qualified as a hurricane, and, as a result, it became known in meteorological circles as simply the Escuminac Hurricane.

As of 2007, Captain Theodore Williston, at the age of 76, is the last surviving captain to have carried out a rescue mission in the Escuminac salmon fishing disaster. He was 28 at the time. Unlike most of the fleet that fateful night in June, he had gone farther out in the strait, fishing mackerel.

"That meant we were outside the salmon fleet, and that's what probably saved us," Theodore explains, pointing out that in those days they fished for mackerel using the same drifting technique that was employed by the salmon fishermen. "I'd say maybe about half of the salmon fleet was out that night. It had been a bad week, weather wise—blowing and cold. I remember it was really miserable. The night before, a Thursday, I told the boys that we would stay in and have a rest. If the weather was good, I told them we'd go out Friday night."

With his two crew members, Aquila Manuel and Larry Martin, on board, Theodore left the Escuminac wharf sometime between 5:00 and 6:00 in the evening. He recalls that the forecast was for northeast, 20-mile [30-kilometre-per-hour] winds with drizzle.

"The system that was bringing the bad weather was supposed to move out to sea and subside. Lows and highs move from west and east, and, in this case, this system was supposed to move east, but instead it backtracked and went west and intensified," he says. "There really is no way to predict these things. It's just nature doing her thing. We had no idea what was coming our way. We went out and headed east for about two hours. I believe we may have actually been closer to Prince Edward Island than we were to the Escuminac point. We set our nets, and, as soon as darkness fell, the weather shut down on us and the wind picked up."

Theodore says at that point he knew there was going to be a blow, but he had no idea how bad it was going to get.

"But it didn't matter. We were there, and we were going on the strength of the forecast from all week. We didn't think it was going to get much worse. If we had, none of the boats would have gone out. We would not have taken the chance knowing the circumstances as they turned out. We had no electronics on our boats at that time. There was no radar, GPS, or radios. In fact, very few boats even had an AM radio on board to pick up the weather forecasts. We just didn't know what was coming."

The three-man crew rode out the storm throughout the night, because, as he says, "Once the storm hit, there was no going back in. It was a bad night. There were high seas. We couldn't sleep. We kept watch all night, constantly checking for water. Along with the waves, it was raining pretty hard, and we knew we had to keep her dry, or we might be swamped. We had to tighten the riding sail a number of times during the night. In such a gale, if that sail starts flapping, then you might lose it, and, if you lost it, it meant big trouble. We kept watch on things until daylight, and we got through it."

When morning came, Theodore says they pulled in their nets and thanked the Lord there had been few fish in the haul because in such high seas, they didn't want to be heavy with a catch.

"It was hard pulling in those nets, and I told the boys that when the sea wants the nets, give them to it. Don't try to hold it. The last thing I needed was for one of them to be swept overboard," Theodore explains. " It was a slow procedure, but we managed to get them in okay, and then we set sail for Escuminac just after daylight."

As a young man, Theodore had fished with his uncle, and he had received a lot of advice.

> *"I remember him telling me that when you get in a bad time, don't come in;* [instead,] *get yourself out to sea to get stable and get your bearings. But on this day, I really didn't heed his advice. I should have, but I didn't. One thing he did tell me though, that I did follow, was that in a storm or fog, if you're not sure of your course, always steer north. We always come in from the west, so if we took a few degrees northwest, this would likely clear us from the Escuminac breakwater and all the rocky shoals. That way, if we did get into trouble, from there north is all sandy beaches, and that would have been a better place to come ashore than the rocks. That advice saved my neck, because, on this morning, there was no visibility—so I did just exactly what my uncle had advised."*

A short time after pulling in the nets and setting course to the north, Theodore encountered another mackerel fisherman, Roy Lloyd. "He was still hanging onto his nets. He told me he was waiting for the weather to subside and the seas to calm done before heading in. His only worry was that his 13-year-old son, Brian, was with him, and Roy knew his wife would be worrying about the boy. I asked him if there was anything he needed. The only thing he asked was that when I got back could I tell his wife that they were okay and that Brian was okay and they'd be in when things calmed down."

With that, Theodore and his crew kept going.

"Once we sailed so far, we kept taking soundings to record our progress. That would tell us when the water was getting shallower. We got to the point where the water was getting real shoal, and I didn't know where I was. I knew I had to turn back, because the sea was breaking, so I knew there were rocks there. I watched for my chance, and, when things were calm, I turned the boat around and headed out through the breakers to the open sea and to deeper water. We kept going, and, after a while…I saw some traps that I knew to be the gear that fishermen on the other side of the bay used. Then I knew where I was. I knew I was on the [salmon] line, and it gave me a pretty good idea where I was headed," he notes.

From that point, Theodore set course for Escuminac.

"I was just running slow, letting the sea take me there. We spied three other boats coming in the same direction that we had just come from, and I knew they'd be in trouble if they went in there, so me and the other crew members waved them down and had them follow us. It wasn't long before we came upon a boat that was in trouble. We ran up alongside—maybe 15 or 20 feet [4.5 or 6 metres] from them. When we did, a rogue sea came up, lifted this fellow's boat up, swung it around in our direction—and it almost came down on us," Theodore recounts. "We managed to get a line to them after another pass or two, and then we towed her along with us."

Suddenly, Theodore says, they watched in horror as one of the other boats that was following along behind was picked up by the sea and tossed over like it was a toy. "It was one of the biggest and newest boats in the fleet. One of the other boats quickly went alongside them, and we watched as they pulled three men out of the water. There wasn't anything we could do. We were already towing a boat. We counted as they pulled the men from the water, and we thought everything was okay, but we didn't know there had been a fourth man on board. That fellow was lost…We felt bad about that," Theodore recalls.

At that point, the other captains turned away and went to deeper seas, remembering the same advice that Theodore's uncle had imparted to him. As well, the captain of the boat they were towing managed to get his engine going, and he joined the other boats.

"It was then that we encountered an awful lot of destruction and a debris field. We came across parts from other boats, things that had been washed overboard, like washboards [planks used to keep the water out], nets, equipment. The debris was in a rip tide, and we knew this wasn't a good sign. When we saw this, that's when we knew things were bad. Luckily, my crew was watching where we were going through this stuff, and we got through the debris, and then, all of a sudden, one of the boys began yelling that he could see a man standing in the water," Theodore continues. "I told him it couldn't possibly be, but then we all saw him, and we knew that despite the danger, we had to go see if there was anything we could do to help this guy."

Sure enough, Theodore says, when they got to the location where the man had been spotted, they found a boat that had been swamped in the high seas, and the man was standing in the back. "We went up alongside to see if there was anything we could do to help. There was no cabin or anything. We could tell it had been hit hard. That's when we saw the man's helper lying on the stern."

Theodore recognized the captain, an older man named Walter Williston, a distant relative of his. The young helper was Harold Taylor, who he knew couldn't have been any more than 20 years of age.

"'Is he dead?' I asked Walter." Walter confirmed that he was.

"I told Walter that we would throw him a line and get him on board. The sea was really rough there, and we wanted to get away from that location as fast as we could, but Walter said the young boy had to go first. He had promised the boy he would get him home."

Walter untied the boy's body, secured him to a line from Theodore's boat and brought the boy on board. Then they made another pass and pulled Walter on board. "It was a numb feeling to have that young boy on board. We felt pretty bad for him. I knew him, and I knew his mother. She was a widow, and I knew this was going be hard on her."

By this time, Theodore and his crew were alone, the other boats having disappeared, most of them heading out to deeper water. That's when he decided they were going to set sail for the Escuminac breakwater. "It was breaking so bad at the Escuminac shore that the only way you could tell it was a breakwater was because the spray was flying higher than anywhere else along the coast, so I knew that must be the breakwater or the wharf. We managed to get in okay all in one piece, but that's when you realized how bad the storm had been. When we heard about all the boats that were missing and the men that were reported drowned, it gave me a numb feeling all over. I had relatives and a really good friend that drowned that morning. And I think, today, it bothers me even more than it did back in 1959," Theodore admits.

That same Friday night, 13-year-old Brian Lloyd wanted to go out with his father, Roy Lloyd, because he hoped he would catch a few cod. In 1959, cod sold for 1.5 cents per pound (3.3 cents per kilogram; that would be 24 cents per kilogram in 2007 money), and he could make a few dollars if he had a good night. He remembers the storm very well. His father had anchored some 12 to 14 kilometres out from shore, because they were going to drift for mackerel.

"We were up half the night. It was a rough sea, but somehow we managed to escape any damage. Many of the boats weren't as lucky."

Unlike Theodore Williston, the next morning Roy Lloyd decided to keep his nets in the water for balance, and they rode out the high waves, staying adrift for several hours throughout much of the morning. It wasn't until later in the afternoon when they made their way in to shore that they learned of the extent of the disaster.

Brian remembers that along the way they encountered a long debris field floating in the waves, and they knew that something terrible must have happened. They found washboards, gas cans, nets—the sort of items that would come from boats.

Suddenly, Brian says, one of the crew members reported seeing a man off to the right of their location. "We made our way towards him. I'd say it took us maybe 20 minutes to half an hour to reach him. We had to work our way through the rough seas, and it took time. When we got to him, we saw that he was tied to the mast. We later learned that he and his father were from Prince Edward Island, and they had been on their boat when the storm hit," he explains. "His father had tied the young man to the mast to keep him from being washed overboard in the high waves."

Brian recalls that the young man was 20 years old, and he was in pretty bad shape when they found him. Sadly, the other man was gone, presumably drowned in the heavy waves.

"There he was, all by himself, tied to the mast that had broken off about 2 feet [60 centimetres] above his head. It seemed to us he was near death. He was in pretty bad shape," he adds. "The boat kept rolling over, and it took the young guy with it each time. The boat would turn under, and he'd go under with it, then he'd come back up again. I remember Dad yelling at him, but he couldn't get any response. The fellow couldn't communicate with us."

Later, Brian continues, they learned that the men's
boat had been swamped around midnight, which meant
that this fellow had been tied to the mast for quite some
time. It was now 2:00 in the afternoon. No wonder he
was near death. Brian says it was a miracle he was still
alive.

Somehow, the crew on Roy's boat got a life jacket to
the young man, and they managed to pull him on board
their boat. "They carried him right down to the cabin to
warm him up, and I remember thinking, 'This guy is
dead. There's no way he could be alive after that pound-
ing,'" Brian explains. But he was alive. "We brought him
back to shore with us," he concludes.

Walter Williston was a seasoned fisherman. When he
and 20-year-old Harold Taylor headed out to sea that Friday
night, no one expected the weather to turn bad. "It was
foggy and breezy, but there was nothing to tell us how
bad it was going to get. When we got up the next morning [Saturday], it was bad. The seas were high, and the
wind was picking up," Walter begins. "We tried to get in
closer to Escuminac wharf, but we got caught up in the
breakers, and then we were in trouble. We started to head
for land when a rogue sea hit us, and we upset."

Walter says it was impossible to see the shoal in such
conditions. "The wind was in, and there was a big tide.
All of a sudden, the boat was swamped. There wasn't any
warning. It cleaned the cutty [cabin] and wheelhouse
completely off the boat. The floor came out of her. It was
pretty bad. We got up on the bow and hoped someone
would come along. That's all we could do."

Stranded on the bow of their disabled and quickly
sinking vessel, the waves hitting them full force, Walter
told Harold that they had to get to the stern. He figured

there was a better chance of that part of the boat remaining above water.

"We managed to get back to the stern by going along the washboard," he recalls. "It was tough going. The seas were hitting us pretty hard. I told the young fellow to hang on. Then I got a rope, put it around him and tied him to the stern post. Every time the sea would wash over us, he'd go down in the hold, and I'd pull him back up. We got beat around pretty good."

Walter says he tried everything he could think of to keep them both alive, but, sadly, Harold couldn't hang on. Before he died, the younger man told Walter he was worried about what his death would do to his mother, who was a widow. "I remember him saying to me at one point that he didn't think we were going to make it ashore, and I told him that we would. I told him not to give up, to keep on fighting. I told him if I get there, you'll get there, but he died...I think the only thing that saved me was that I had lots of clothes on, and that helped to insulate me against the cold."

He says it's hard to describe how cold he was in that water. "I don't think I've been that cold ever again in my life. I was cold through and through, right to the bone."

In total, Walter says he was in the water about four and a half hours from the time his boat was swamped until he saw Theodore's boat coming towards him. "By the time the fog lifted and I could see his boat coming to me, I could also see how close we were to shore, and that's when the young boy's death really hit me...We were so close, but we just couldn't make it. I could actually see the picnic tables that were on the beach. I could see the breakwater pretty plain from where I was. I just couldn't get to it. But I knew that if I had left the boat, I would have died too. I just thought it best that I stay there and wait for someone to come along," Walter elaborates. "I knew that somebody would see me sooner or later."

By the time Theodore brought his ship within range, Walter says he was pretty tired and beat up. "It was a tough time. They threw me a rope, and I put it on the young fellow first, and they hauled him aboard. I told them that I promised him he'd come home with me, and he did. I wasn't leaving him there...I just couldn't. Then they came around again and threw me a rope and pulled me on board. I was safe, but I sure felt bad about the young fellow. He was a neighbour that I had known all his life, but there was nothing I could do. We can't change things like that," he concedes. "It was just meant to be."

Despite his harrowing ordeal, Walter says he never considered getting out of fishing. "I missed a week of the season that year, then I went and rented a boat and went back out. I fished the rest of the season and the rest of my life until I retired. It's all we could do. I really had no choice. I had a family to take care of, and there wasn't anything else around here to work at," he says with a shrug. "It's what I had to do."

⚬⟨❖⟩⚬

The Escuminac tragedy touched the entire Atlantic region. On June 24, 1959, headlines across the country told the story. The *Lunenburg Progress-Enterprise* spread the news in Nova Scotia, a place not immune to seafaring disasters. The headline screamed in big, bold letters: "32 Fishermen Are Missing When Gales Hit New Brunswick Coast." The following story appeared beneath it:

> *"Fifty fishing boats were caught in the worst storm disaster ever to hit the Gulf of St. Lawrence last week. Thirteen bodies have been recovered, and nineteen have been officially listed as missing. It is feared, however,*

that the toll will be greater as the search continues in the smaller hamlets along the shore.

Besides the loss of life, the damage to fishing boats and gear will be heavy when waves up to 50 feet [15 metres] high rolled along the Northumberland Strait.

"Most of the fishermen lost are from the Escuminac and Bay Ste. Anne [sic] and Baie Du Vin [sic] areas, and damage to property reaches south as far as Shediac, where summer cottages were lashed by the heavy sea.

"The salmon was running well, and the fishermen hurried to reap a good catch. The storm was unexpected and caught the fleet on the fishing grounds with no time to take shelter.

"In many cases, father and son were lost, as well as brothers, who operated boats together. Families of missing men have been on the shores watching hopefully for the return of their loved ones. The RCAF and RCMP were on the scene as soon as the storm subsided and are continuing the search.

The Red Cross moved in[to] the area as soon as word of distress was received and established headquarters at Escuminac."

A monument with an inscription carved in both official languages now stands on the shores of Escuminac Harbour to honour the 35 men who were lost that June in 1959. The storm was a dark chapter in the history of New Brunswick.

Bell Island Boom

April 2, 1978
The Avalon Peninsula, Newfoundland

THE BELL ISLAND BOOM OCCURRED on April 2, 1978. a large explosion and disruption, it damaged many homes in the vicinity of Bell Island, which is located off the Avalon Peninsula of Newfoundland.

Bell Island was first settled by Englishman Gregory Normore in 1740. We can only imagine that the strange things in nature that he must have encountered during his first winter alone on the isle would surely have paled in comparison with the unusual and unexplained event that would descend upon the residents of Bell Island more than 200 years later.

The cause of the explosion has been a topic of debate ever since. Although the blast caused no fatalities, it did produce significant property damage and created two or three cup-shaped holes in the rocky ground. These holes were reported to be between 60 and 90 centimetres in width and 60 centimetres deep. The blast was heard 45 kilometres away, and American Vela satellites (which were designed to detect nuclear explosions) are said to have picked up the event.

Bell Island is only about 34 square kilometres in size and lies in Conception Bay. It is a 20-minute drive, followed by a 20-minute ferry ride, from St. John's. The isle's famed iron ore mine, known as the No. 2 Mine, closed in 1949, but for years it boosted the local economy, with a total of 80 million tonnes of ore having been extracted during 71 years of mining operations on the island. It was, for a time, the British Commonwealth's largest producer of iron ore. Today, the mine is a tourist attraction.

Interestingly, Bell Island was among the few places in North America to see, firsthand, the ramifications of wartime combat during World War II when, in 1942, German U-boats torpedoed a pier loaded with iron ore, taking out four other vessels in the process. Upwards of 81,000 tonnes of ore had been stored at the pier and was awaiting shipment. a total of 69 people died during the two attacks; they are commemorated by a seamen's memorial located at Lance Cove at the southern end of the island.

Although Bell Island had its days of excitement during World War II, the "boom" some 36 years after Nazis roamed the coastline also proved disturbing. Initially, it was blamed on a phenomenon known as "ball lightning." However, according to Tom Bearden, a retired colonel and nuclear engineer who conducted extensive research on the history of electromagnetic weapons research, the Bell Island Boom of April 1978 may represent unsettling technological experiments.

The incident occurred in the Bickfordville area, which is located on the southwestern side of the island. According to what Bearden found, an unusual beam of what locals believed was lightning came directly down (not jagged like lightning usually is) from the sky at a 45-degree angle to the ground. Strangely, most metal items that would usually be struck by lightning were left untouched. However, the "lightning" vaporized wires leading to a nearby shed, and that structure, along with a nearby chicken coop, suffered damage, but there was no evidence of burning consistent with most types of known lightning strikes. In addition, a number of television sets in the nearby settlement at Lance Cove reportedly exploded at the time of the supposed lightning strike.

The event attracted American scientists from a weapons research facility in Los Alamos and led to speculation that the American military may have been testing some sort of electromagnetic-based weapon over Newfoundland during this Cold War–era event, Bearden notes. Meteorological reports at the time that indicate atmospheric conditions on that April day in 1978 were not conducive to the development of lightning over the Avalon Peninsula.

A local source says that the holes left behind by the mysterious event are still evident in the ground today, nearly 30 years later.

Sinking of the *Ocean Ranger*

THE LAST MEMORY SAMANTHA GERBEAU has of her father, Guy Gerbeau, is of the two of them driving down an open highway—somewhere—when they quickly come upon another vehicle in the lane in front of them; it was moving much slower than their car, slowing their progress.

"Don't worry, Samantha," Guy says to her in her memory. He was an impatient man, she recalls. "We'll get around this," he tells her.

Without hesitation, Guy pulls his car out into the other lane and quickly speeds past the second vehicle. Within minutes, the other car is out of sight. But the episode remains an important part of Samantha's long-term memories.

"Just like that," she recalls years later. "Without a second thought, he was around that car in a flash, and away we went...It was those little things that I remember about him, such as his zest for life, his desire to seize the moment. He wasn't waiting for that car. No sir. I don't remember where we were going, but I know he was in a hurry to get there."

Samantha Gerbeau was only 11 years old at the time of the tragedy, but she remembers the day—February 15, 1982—quite clearly, for it was the date that changed her life forever.

"Yes, I remember it," she begins. "I remember it very well, every little detail, because it was the day I lost him. It was the day that my father left my life forever. How do you ever forget that?...You don't."

Samantha recalls that the day before, Valentine's Day, it had snowed hard, and Newfoundland was buried beneath mountainous drifts, some as high as houses. "In fact, it had been snowing very hard that entire winter. It was a terrible winter. There was snow everywhere, and the storm on February 14 seemed particularly bad," she adds. It was so intense that the mayor of St. John's at the time, John Murphy, had called for all the schools to be closed the next day.

For a youngster like Samantha, that was terrific news. "I loved snow days," she laughs, quickly adding, "What kid doesn't like a day off school? But the excitement was even better with this storm because they actually announced before we went to bed that night that schools were going to be closed the next day. What could be better than that? I remember that I went to bed very excited that evening."

Knowing that she had no school the next day, Samantha made plans to keep busy. Instead of sleeping in, as many students do when they're sprung from classes by a severe winter storm, she was up by around 7:00 that morning. "One of my favourite pastimes was cleaning and rearranging my bedroom, and that's what I decided to do on this snow day. I started cleaning and moving things around. I remember dragging a television set out from the living room and into my bedroom so I could watch cartoons while I was cleaning."

While going about her chores, Samantha had found one of her favourite cartoons, *Spider-Man*, on the CBC and was busily enjoying the morning when things suddenly changed. In an instant, her world came crashing down upon her. Without warning, she says she remembers that they interrupted the show with an urgent news bulletin about an accident on one of the oil rigs. "Glen Tilley, who was an announcer on the CBC news at the time, came on and said, 'We interrupt this program for this special news bulletin. We have just had word that the *Ocean Ranger* has sunk.'"

Samantha says although she knew the news was important, she had not yet connected it with her father. "I really had no idea what the *Ocean Ranger* was," she admits. "I knew my father was away working, but I had no idea where he was, and I surely didn't think that this had anything to do with him, but this sounded pretty important, so I thought I should go tell my mother."

Because it was still just past 7:00 in the morning, and much of the activity in the province had been stalled by the storm, Samantha's mother was still sleeping.

"I remember going into her room and waking her with the news," Samantha recalls. "I said, 'Mom, I don't know what's happening, but the man on the TV said something called the *Ocean Ranger* has just sunk.'"

Samantha remembers that her mother's reaction was immediate and urgent. "She sat up in the bed like a bolt of lightning. 'Oh my God!' she screamed. 'Your father's on that!' I was freaking out by then, and, from that point on, things went from crazy to worse."

As the news of the *Ocean Ranger* sinking spread across the island, she says, "All hell broke loose. It was horrible...really horrible. This was just an awful thing for an 11-year-old child to have to face. I remember the first thing I did when I found out that my father was on that rig was to pray that he would somehow be okay. I always missed him so much when he was away working, but now I had to face the unthinkable," Samantha explains. "I had to accept that I might never see him again."

The next few days were a blur, she says, quickly adding that as the weeks and months went by, things never really improved all that much. The phone rang off the hook and news reports and chaos filled the house. Emotions ran high as everyone was down to their last nerve. "I was only a child. It was just me and Mom at home that morning. We were so shaken by this news. The most that we could do was pray that he would be okay, that somehow—by some miracle—he had been able to survive the tragedy. I honestly figured it would just be a matter of time before my father would be rescued, and that he would tell us about getting off the rig and floating to safety," she goes on. "No one at that age would be able to think that something so tragic could happen to them."

It would be days, even weeks, until her hope started to fade, before she would give up and eventually accept the unthinkable. "I prayed that he would be found, and I lived with that helpless feeling for two weeks, hanging onto even the smallest shred of hope that he would be rescued...But he never was."

In time, Samantha began to accept that she would never see her father again, that he was no longer a part of her life, except in her memories. Now, all these years later, she can tell her story with hardly any trace of emotion in her voice, but she admits it took her a long time to get to that point. One of her prized possessions is an aging photo of her father. It is a company snapshot sent to her shortly after the disaster. In it, Guy Gerbeau looks out of the picture, smiling and tanned, wearing his derrickman's coveralls. He appears every bit the "lively, adventurous type" his daughter remembers him being:

> *"I was pretty angry for a very long time after that night. I lived for several years after the accident filled with anger and hatred and thinking how unjust it was that he was taken from me for no good reason, at least*

*for no reason that I could understand. I think I was old
enough to know what was happening around me, but
I didn't understand the full complexity behind it. My
mother spent the next two years of her life battling with
the courts for settlements. It was such an unhappy time
for us. It wasn't about money for us, because no amount
of money would replace my father, but this was the rage
of it all. Within a very short time, the tragedy seemed to
become more about the money than about the lost lives
and the men who died out there. That seemed so wrong
to me at the time, and it seems so wrong to me even
today."*

The day after the disaster, wanting to be around her
friends, Samantha went to school. She thought it was
important to maintain her routine. That's when she began
to see how big this disaster really was. "I remember that
when I went into school that next day, the auditorium was
filled, and they had a moment of silence for all the people
who had died on the rig. It wasn't until then that I realized
what an impact this had on everybody."

It seemed that the tragedy had practically touched the
entire province. Of the 84 men on board the *Ocean Ranger*
and lost when it went down, 69 were Canadian, of which
56 were Newfoundlanders.

Ray Guy, in an article in the *Sunday Express* following
the sinking, called it, "The great silent moan that arose
from one end of the province to the other."

At the time, the *Ocean Ranger* tragedy was the world's
second-worst offshore drilling catastrophe (the 1980 collapse of the *Alexander Kielland* platform off Norway killed
123 of 212 workers), a position that it would retain until
1988, when the *Piper Alpha* would go up in flames off
Scotland, killing 167 of 229 workers. The *Ocean Ranger's*
demise may not have slowed the petroleum industry in
Newfoundland, but it did remind those involved of the

dangers that come with it. It was a brutal wake-up call to the industry.

The *Ocean Ranger* was designed by ODECO Engineers of New Orleans. Promoted as the biggest rig in the world and weighing more than 14,000 tonnes, the *Ocean Ranger* was built by Mitsubishi Heavy Industries in Hiroshima, Japan. It first saw use in 1976, in the Bering Sea off Alaska. In the following years, it was moved to New Jersey and then Ireland. In November 1980, leased to Mobil Oil for $93,000 per day, it arrived on the Grand Bank amid much fanfare as politicians heralded its arrival as the beginning of a new era for Newfoundland—the era of oil. Considered unsinkable and permitted "unrestricted" operation in any waters, the *Ocean Ranger* was a massive oil rig—the largest of its kind.

Brian Bursey, a retired teacher living in St. John's, Newfoundland, was 29 years of age when the *Ocean Ranger* toppled over into the stormy seas of the Atlantic Ocean sometime around 1:00 in the morning of February 15, 1982, taking its full crew with it. His brother, Paul, was one those men who perished in the frigid, unforgiving waters that night.

Paul was 30 years old when he died in the tragedy, and Brian says he has never been able to shake the feeling that he had been robbed of something precious to him. Being close to each other in age, the Bursey brothers had practically been inseparable as children and teenagers. Although they had an older sibling—Wayne—Brian and Paul were tight. "As we got older and pursued our careers, we went in different directions but always maintained contact. I went off to chase a teaching career, and he went off to become an electrician, something he was very good at, but we always kept in touch."

This picture was taken on board the *Ocean Ranger* sometime during 1981. It shows Paul Bursey, in his job as an electrician, checking some of the rig's electrical operations.

At the time of his death, Paul was still single and living at home with their widowed mother. "She had grown to depend upon him a great deal, especially with me and Wayne out of the house. Paul had spent a few years working in Alberta, but he came back home and moved into the house with our mother to take care of things. There was a fair amount of dependence on Paul from her part. This made it extremely difficult for us to deal with Paul's death. When I moved out after I got married, Paul lived with her for a while, and they became close. It was a terrible blow to her when he died. It was something that she could never get over," Brian explains. "It was something that, when she died at the age of 70, she took to the grave with her. She talked about it all the time. It never went away. I think that's only natural. I'm sure the loss of a child, no matter how old they are, is very difficult for a parent to deal with. She never let go of Paul."

In truth, Brian admits it was hard for the entire family to let go of him. "Losing someone is never easy, but losing someone under such disastrous circumstances is even more difficult. There were so many questions and no answers following the sinking. The families were just left hanging, and no one was held accountable."

Reflecting upon his brother's death, Brian says the irony of the situation serves as a stark reminder that life is extremely unpredictable and that nothing should ever be taken for granted.

"When Paul died, he had only been on the rig for less than a year," he says. "And the sad part about all of this is that when the rig went down, Paul was on his last shift out there. Before going back out to start that shift, he actually had purchased a plane ticket to go back out West to take another job. He wanted to give Alberta another try, because he thought the money was better. If this tragedy had happened a few weeks later, he would not have been there."

The last memory Brian has of Paul is a conversation the brothers shared about working on the *Ocean Ranger* and Paul's reservations regarding its safety:

> "*We had talked many times about the situation out there, and he didn't think it was good. The rig had a bad reputation, and it had already experienced some difficulty in the months prior to its sinking. The men had a feeling something wasn't right. He talked about the crew being ill prepared in the event of a problem on board the rig. The* Ocean Ranger *had gone into a serious list at one time, but they righted it, and no one seemed to be worried. It bothered Paul that just because they believed that this was the mighty* Ocean Ranger, *nothing could happen to it. They* [both the employees

and company officials] *really believed it was invincible. We talked about that and about the fact that safety didn't seem to be a real issue of concern for the company."*

However, Brian says, Paul was philosophical about the situation. "He said he was only there for a short term, and he didn't want to be the one to cause a fuss. That would be Paul. He said he would be gone after this last shift, and he would not have to worry about it after that. But he certainly didn't feel safe out there. It didn't appear that safety was highly regarded on the rig. There was an attitude that there was no need to worry, because if the rig was as good as everyone said it was, then there was nothing that the force of nature could throw against it," Brian notes. "There really was a false feeling that the *Ocean Ranger* could withstand anything."

Obviously, Brain adds, his brother and all the others connected with the rig were wrong.

Brian first learned of the catastrophe by listening to the radio news. "We hadn't heard anything about it. No one called to tell us there was a problem, not even the company Paul worked for."

Indeed, Brian pointed out during this interview, even to January 2007, just a month before the 25th anniversary of the tragedy, the families had never officially been contacted by anyone from the company offering an explanation or expressing sympathies. Although the families all received a form letter saying how sorry the company was, he believes it could have done better than that. He believes the company should have reached out to the families, but there was not much in the way of communication or explanation.

On the morning of February 15, he had no idea of the reality that would soon become his life. "Truthfully, the first we heard that there was a problem on board the *Ocean Ranger* was when we turned on the radio for the early morning news to see if school had been cancelled because of the snow," he explains. "As a teacher, I was listening to see if I had to drive into work that day. I had a long commute. As it turned it out, classes had been cancelled, but that was the furthest thing from my mind."

However, even with the newscast, Brian recalls the family still didn't know much. "Then my mom phoned and said she had just heard that *Ocean Ranger* had experienced some trouble throughout the night because of the storm, and the word was that it was listing pretty badly and that the men were being taken to the lifeboats. Of course, hearing that still made you think that we had heard about that sort of thing before, and that everybody would be fine. We thought Paul would be safe."

Regardless, the news was still upsetting to his elderly mother, so Brian promised that he would find out what was happening and get back to her. He told her not worry. Brian says he knew his older brother, Wayne, had some contacts with the Coast Guard in St. John's, and he hoped they would be able to give the family some news.

"Instead of calling, Wayne and I decided to go the Coast Guard office to talk to them in person. We figured if anyone would have an inside track on this thing, it would be the Coast Guard," Brian continues. "When we first got there, however, they weren't exactly forthcoming. I guess we should have expected that. Eventually, though, we met up with my brother's contact, and he took us into his office. There was something about the expression on his face that we knew something was wrong. We could tell that he knew more than we did. Finally, he asked us if we knew anything, and we assured him that the only information we heard was what they had reported on the news. We told him we had tried to reach the company, but that didn't get us anywhere."

Brian says the Coast Guard official stalled for a few minutes, then bluntly delivered the terrible news to the brothers.

"There's never any good way to say something like this. He comes across the desk and delivers the blow to us. He tells us that the rig was not listing at a 15- or 18-degree angle like the news had said. He bluntly told us that there no longer was an *Ocean Ranger,* that the rig was long since gone. He said that some of the men had reportedly taken to the lifeboats, but the possibility of any survivors was almost nil." Brian pauses, gathers his thoughts, then continues. "It was just unbearable for us to hear that type of news. The next thing we knew we had to do was to figure out what to do with it. We wondered how best to break the news to our mother. We knew it would be devastating to her."

Later that day, with the help of some members from their church, the brothers eventually delivered the bad news; their mother took it hard, as they knew she would.

Although there are reports of the crew referring to the rig as the "Ocean Danger," the industry considered it to be the safest drilling platform on the water. "It had a kind of *Titanic* reputation," says Craig Squires of St. John's, who spent eight months working on the rig as a weather observer, while speaking to Stephanie Porter, a reporter for the *Express* weekly newspaper. "We were told it was the 'Unsinkable *Ocean Ranger.*' It was designed for use anywhere in the world, in every weather condition."

The *Ranger* was one of three semisubmersible rigs—all under contract to Mobil Oil Canada—drilling at the time on the Hibernia oilfield, about 200 kilometres east of St. John's. The structure consisted of a drilling platform held in place by huge anchors that rested on two pontoons that floated just below the surface of the water. Each was longer than a football field. To stabilize the immense rig, 24 ballast tanks and six pumps were contained in the pontoons. By pumping seawater in and out of the tanks, the ballast operator could keep the rig level while loading equipment from a supply ship—or during rough weather.

On Sunday, February 14, an especially fierce storm that had begun in the Gulf of Mexico was strengthening off the coast of Newfoundland. By late that day, the winds in the Hibernia oilfield had reached hurricane force, and the short but tall waves, which averaged 15 metres in height, sometimes reached as high as 27 metres; a storm of this magnitude can be expected only about once a decade. Sometime after 7:00, the *Ocean Ranger* reported that a massive wave had hit the rig and burst a porthole in the ballast control room. The salt water shorted out the control and monitoring circuits. With the crew now powerless to effectively control the pumps and valves, the rig began to list. The rig began to take on water, worsening the list. At five minutes past one on Sunday morning, February 15, the crew requested that the supply ship MV *Seaforth Highlander* approach and stand by to help if necessary.

Four minutes later, the *Ocean Ranger* sent an SOS signal. "We're listing badly, and we need to get the seamen off the rig," it said. "We may not be able to hold the rig, rig might fall over," said a subsequent message.

At half past one, in its final message, the *Ocean Ranger* indicated that the crew was taking to the lifeboats. By 2:00 AM, nearby oil-rig supply boats arrived in the area and attempted to save the crew. Unfortunately, they were ill equipped for such a mission, especially with such rough weather, and not a single person of the 84 was rescued alive. Shortly after 3:30 that morning, Coast Guard and other would-be rescuers watched their radars in utter horror and disbelief as the *Ocean Ranger* vanished.

Search teams combing the area over the next four days retrieved 22 bodies, two lifeboats and six life rafts.

Launched within months of the *Ocean Ranger*'s demise, a Royal Commission that deliberated on the disaster for over two years concluded that design flaws, especially in the ballast control room, led to the sinking. Further, it stated, had the crew been supplied with proper training and safety equipment, many of the workers might have survived. In all, the report made 136 suggestions to improve the safety and accountability of the industry, including the need for tougher federal safety and inspection standards for rigs; improved worker safety, emergency response planning and training; design changes and increased competency among industry workers.

As a result of the *Ocean Ranger* sinking, the government acted to improve the safety of the offshore oil workers, and industry rules are now better enforced. One such rule requires workers to present a current safety certification card prior to being allowed to board a helicopter to the rig. Along with better safety training, workers are now provided with cold-water survival suits. The methods for deploying lifeboats have also improved, and weather forecasting has advanced as well, in part because of additional monitoring buoys in the region.

The families of the dead sought legal action against Mobil Oil Canada and ODECO. Because they had not provided adequate emergency training and survival equipment, the companies were found to be liable for the 84 deaths. Had the crewmembers been properly trained in the operation of the ballast system, they could have prevented the capsizing. Had they been supplied with proper survival gear, they would have stood a better chance of surviving. The companies paid out millions of dollars in settlements as a result.

Although changes designed to prevent a repeat of the *Ocean Ranger* disaster have been made, they are of little comfort to those who lost loved ones on that stormy night in early 1982. Twenty-five years later, people such as Samantha Gerbeau and Brian Bursey still have huge voids in their lives.

"Money just could not replace the love of a parent," Samantha says. "I still had my mother, but I missed my father very much, especially during milestones in my life, like when I got married and had my two children. As I go through life and these wonderful things are happening to me, I wish he were here with me. There is a big hole that is where he's supposed to be. I was so angry for many years, and it was something that I had to work very hard to understand and to come to terms with. It was very, very difficult for me," she recounts.

Eventually, though, Samantha says, she hit a turning point in her life, a point where she knew she had to change things or she would be consumed by the anger.

"I was 28 or 29, and it was right after my daughter was born. I knew that—as a parent—I had to give up the anger. It was extremely unhealthy for me to hang onto all that anger and these feelings of injustice. I know I still carry a part of it deep down inside of me, and I think I always will. It's a part of me. I have this feeling that letting go entirely would be like letting go of him, and I can't do that. I feel I owe it to him to keep remembering, but I also know there are things in my life that I have to take care of and deal with. Once I told myself to let go of the anger, I've been able to deal with things, and I did start to feel better," she explains.

Because her father's body was never recovered, Samantha says there has never been any real closure for her. "If they had found him, and we could have given him a proper burial, then maybe I would have felt differently over the years, but there has never been any ending to this nightmare for us."

Even the plaque commemorating the tragedy and remembering the men who died on the *Ocean Ranger* caused her considerable grief—her father's name was incorrectly spelled. Samantha waged a battle that lasted several years and took her all the way to the premier's office, but eventually the name was fixed. "It hit me hard every time I looked at that plaque. I had to have it changed in honour of his memory. I know he's gone from the earth, but I believe he's still here all around me. I just feel him even today, 25 years later."

Her father's legacy, Samantha says, is the changes that have come from the tragedy. "He, and all those other men, paid a huge sacrifice to save thousands of lives around the world. When I started perceiving my loss on that level, everything else seemed to go away. The whole thing—the pain, the injustice, the anger—it all went away. I have to think that he and the others didn't die in vain. I'm not sure if the family members were ever really satisfied with what became of things, or if they just reached a point where they had had enough," she concludes.

Brian agrees. After a while, people reach a point where they cannot take it anymore. The body begins to shut down, he says. "One would like to think that some of the things that came from the inquiry, such as the safety regulations, might be used to prevent another tragedy, but I'm never really convinced of that. Even with everything that they said was done to make improvements, we still live with a lot of doubts. Everything was supposed to be so great with the *Ocean Ranger*, but look at what happened. It makes you wonder about the structures that are out there today and wonder just how safe they are. Do they have some little design flaw that Mother Nature could be able to unravel? She did it with the *Ocean Ranger*, and it was supposed to be invincible," Brian observes. "God forbid that anything like that should ever happen again, but it's always there in the back of my mind, just as it is with other family members, I'm sure."

Tragedies at sea are a way of life in Atlantic Canada, Brian says, and although this catastrophe was never supposed to happen, it did, and there is no way to change the past. Eventually, it is important to accept and to move on.

"Tragedies are a part of our culture as a seafaring nation. Certainly, Newfoundland and the Maritimes can attest to that. We've all lived by the sea, and we've seen a tremendous amount of disaster at sea. It has become part of our way of life, and now we've entered the oil industry into that aspect of our culture. Our economy has been built on the sea, but it can be a dangerous partner. The oil industry is moving ahead in leaps and bounds, and it is offshore based, and that means there will be more and more risks," he concedes.

To prevent future tragedies, Brian says it is important to remember the past events such as the *Ocean Ranger*. "We must never forget. We must make sure the next generation keeps these memories alive. We must learn from our past mistakes, and—above all—we must remember those men who died that night."

Great Ice Storm of 1998

January 5 to 10, 1998
New Brunswick and Nova Scotia

WE SO OFTEN TAKE THE MODERN conveniences of life for granted. The idea that we will have a roof over our heads, cooked food on our tables and a heat source through which to warm our abode is taken as a given by most Canadians, most of the time. Then, there are other days in which the wanton destructive abilities of nature are made abundantly clear. Under nature's sheer power we are reminded, as a species, that we are but guests on this planet and at the whim of its climatological mercies. In 1998, the people of Eastern Canada were given just such a reminder.

The Great Ice Storm, which blasted Eastern Canada from January 5 to 10, 1998, hit eastern Ontario and southern Québec the hardest. Most areas affected by the storm received at least 40 millimetres of freezing rain that formed solid, thick coatings of ice on trees, cars, sidewalks, homes—literally everything under the sky. In localized areas, the accumulations were even higher, ranging any where from 60 to 100 millimetres. The ice load snapped power lines and wooden poles with the greatest of ease. Even the mammoth metal electrical towers scattered across Québec, supposedly built to withstand the worst that nature could muster, crumpled under the weight of the ice as if they were built of matchsticks, leaving millions of people at various intervals huddled in the cold and dark at its worst.

Most areas affected by the Great Ice Storm received at least
40 millimeters of rain, which, under freezing temperatures,
formed solid, thick coatings of ice on trees, cars, sidewalks,
homes—every exposed surface.

The storm had a lesser impact on the Maritimes, bringing upwards of 40 millimetres of freezing rain into parts of southern New Brunswick and on Nova Scotia's Bay of Fundy shoreline. Once the local situation was in hand, teams from all three Maritime provinces responded to calls for assistance from our Canadian brethren along the Montréal–Kingston corridor in Québec and Ontario. Those workers joined with members of the Canadian Armed Forces as part of Operation Recuperation, which saw nearly 16,000 personnel, including almost 3800 reservists, aid in the effort to bring life back to normal following the devastation of the ice storm.

Although the Great Ice Storm of 1998 was not as severe in Atlantic Canada as it had been throughout much of the heavily populated regions of Québec and Ontario, it nonetheless had an impact, bringing everyday life to a screeching halt and reminding us that we are, in spite of any beliefs to the contrary, not so impervious to climate after all. Across the part of Canada hit by the storm, a total of 25 people died as a direct result of it, with many of them succumbing to hypothermia. The storm was also a wake-up call to energy providers on this half of the continent, such as Nova Scotia Power and Hydro-Québec, to make sure that they were better prepared to deal with any future large weather disasters. Homeowners also learned a valuable lesson from the storm, and emergency preparedness subsequently became a top priority throughout the region. As we know, if it happened once, it can happen again.

Part II
Accidental Disasters

Miramichi Fire

October 7, 1825
Miramichi Region of New Brunswick

THE SUMMER OF 1825 WAS one of the hottest on record. Most of North America was in the grip of an extensive heat wave that left much of the landscape parched and longing for a refreshing drink of water to quench its thirst. But the rains did not come. Instead, as the summer wore on, people across the continent suffered the heat's ill effects, with many succumbing to the intense sweltering temperatures. Deaths were reported far and wide.

In Atlantic Canada, the heat wave hit with a vengeance. Fires raged throughout the region, but most hard hit was the province of Nova Scotia, with hectares of forests falling in ashes. By mid-September, however, Nova Scotians longing for relief from the oppressive heat finally got what they prayed for—rain, and lots of it—to quench the earth's thirst. The fires were subsequently extinguished, and all sighed a deep relief. The worst was over, at least for Nova Scotians, but for their neighbours to the north in New Brunswick, the nightmare was just beginning.

Somehow, for most of the summer, except for the occasional flare-up, New Brunswick had miraculously escaped any major fires. Then, as the cooler fall weather arrived, residents counted their blessings and thanked their maker for sparing them any grief. That all changed on the afternoon of October 7, 1825.

Despite the late time of year, that October day was sweltering hot, with temperatures climbing to well above the normal range. Manford Wasson, a retired schoolteacher and president of the Miramichi Historical Society, has made it a passion to study the events of that fall day. "While the rain had begun falling in Nova Scotia and putting out their fires, here in the Miramichi we barely had a drop of water all summer long," he explains. "It was extremely dry in this part of the province. And the woods were just a disaster waiting to happen. They were dry...Very dry."

Based on historical records and data from that period, at about 3:30 in the afternoon, Wasson says that the people of Newcastle and Chatham noticed a dense cloud of smoke on the horizon. "By all accounts, it was way off at a considerable distance northwest of Newcastle," he notes. "But, despite the dry conditions in the forest, no one seemed to be panicked. The wind was moderate, but moving from the north, and as such it appeared to be pushing the fire in that direction."

As long as that trend continued, there was no reason to worry that fire would strike them.

For the remainder of the afternoon and into the early evening, the people of Newcastle and Chatham watched the smoke. They could see the bright orange of the fire light up the evening sky. Then it struck with fervour.

"At about 7:00 in the evening, a breeze sprung up from the northwest," Wasson tells the story. "Almost immediately, ash and cinders started to fly, landing in the towns and causing a great panic. Suddenly, people knew they had a problem, and they took to their houses."

By 8:00 PM, Miramichi residents were brought to a standstill as a loud roaring could be heard throughout the neighbouring towns. Like a flaming monster moving in on its prey, the fire descended upon the town of Newcastle, and its population of roughly 1000 inhabitants was caught in the fire's crosshairs:

"It swooped down from the north, moving rapidly across the treetops and swallowing everything in its path. People fled their homes, some hardly clothed, and sought refuge in the nearby rivers and marshes in hopes of escaping a fiery death. People plunged into the rivers up to their necks to protect their skins while, throughout the town, the anguished cries of domestic animals filled the air as they were suffocated by the thick black smoke or consumed by the flames. Others took to wooden rafts and small boats to escape the quickly advancing flames. Even many of the ships anchored in the harbour were attacked by the fire...Nothing was spared."

It was like hell on earth. There seemed to be no escaping the beast.

The area affected by the Miramichi Fire of 1825 stretched from north of Fredericton to the Baie de Chaleurs. Estimates pegged the total swath at about 16,000 square kilometres, or about one-fifth of New Brunswick. It's possible that five or six large fires simultaneously burning were driven together by the wind. The village of Newcastle, among other areas, was razed. Historians claim that the Miramichi fire of 1825 was, at the time, the largest forest fire in the history of Canada, if not the entire continent. Certainly, it was the largest recorded fire on the eastern seaboard of North America.

Officially, the cause of the Miramichi fire remains unknown, its origins a mystery buried among the ashes. It had been a hot, dry summer in this famous timber district, so there was a lot of natural kindling lying about. Even the exact nature of the blaze, and whether it was one large fire or several smaller ones that combined, has long been a matter of speculation. Attempts, over the years, to determine the cause and true extent have been hampered by the shortage of contemporary accounts of the fire, so blame has been ascribed to several sources.

At the time, the New Brunswick woods were littered with lumbermen as well as the debris from the shaving and squaring of lumber. Lightning is certainly a possible cause of ignition, and it has also been speculated that settlers clearing land may have ignited a blaze that they could not control.

The first sign of trouble was reported in the afternoon of October 7, 1825, which described a large column of smoke clearly visible. By 7:00 PM, flaming debris had been confirmed in the Miramichi near the Chatham and Newcastle region. Chatham and Newcastle lie on opposite sides of the shoreline near the mouth of the Miramichi River in northeastern New Brunswick. The river is roughly 1.5 kilometres wide at that point and is noticeably tidal. Even in its early days, Newcastle–Chatham was a centre known for its lumbering and salmon fishing.

The people who survived the flames would soon be facing a new threat—starvation and exposure to the elements with the arrival of winter. Thousands were left homeless, and many people are reported to have drowned while trying to escape the oncoming flames by jumping into the Miramichi River. The total number of deaths caused by the blaze is impossible to accurately ascertain. It was believed that 160 residents of the Newcastle–Chatham area died, and many more lumbermen and frontier settlers in the surrounding woods are thought to have also perished. There may have been as many as 3000 lumbermen operating in the area. It is believed that many of them died in the flames that day, but their bodies were never recovered. There were no official records of these people, so it is impossible to know for sure how many were lost.

Structural damage was significant. Gone were New-castle's church, barracks, courthouse and 450 residential dwellings. One local newspaper, the Miramichi *Mercury*, reported in 1826, a number of months following the blaze, that not counting the value of the timberland destroyed, the estimated cost of damage caused by the inferno ranged to about 249,000 pounds sterling.

In *Redcoat Sailor,* author R.S. Lambert estimates that 300 people lost their lives in the fire, with as many as 600 buildings being destroyed along the passage from Fredericton northeast to Newcastle. In *These Are the Maritimes,* Will R. Bird estimates that within three min-utes of the first flames being observed near Newcastle, with a strong southwesterly blaze fanning the flames, most homes in the community were lit and burning.

From the damage in the northeast of the province, the fire (or one of its branches) reached all the way to the cap-ital of Fredericton. The King Street area from the inter-section of Carleton to Westmorland (about two blocks) raged with fire, levelling about 70 buildings in total. Whether the Fredericton blaze was completely separate from the one that affected the upper Miramichi region, several hundred kilometres away, or if both areas were hit by parts of a single lengthy wall of fire, no one knows with certainty, but it was certainly the offspring of a summer-long drought in central and northern New Brunswick that produced such dangerous conditions.

New Brunswick Lieutenant Governor Howard Douglas, in the House of Assembly the following January, said, "Here, in the seat of Government, the loss, though great, has mercifully been confined to property, but in other quarters, the conflagration raged with more fatal fury."

Despite a multitude of descriptions depicting the blaze as massive and devastating, Thomas Baillie, the Commissioner of Crown Lands in the province, in a letter written on

October 31, 1825, said that the impact of the fire had been minimal, perhaps in an effort to ensure that the valuable lumbering industry did not suffer from depreciation because of the blaze.

The total cost of the fire is difficult to tabulate, but Manford Wasson said it took years for the region to recover. "In the aftermath, there was a major exodus. After losing everything they owned in the fire, many families from this area went to Québec and Upper Canada. And many of them went to the United States, particularly the states of Wisconsin and Minnesota. It wasn't easy to stay in the Miramichi. Everything was gone, but for those who remained, they survived...They were courageous. They were resilient, and they were self-reliant people. They were not prepared to give in to this tragedy. They rose above it. In time, they recovered from this tremendous blow, and they rebuilt this community from the ashes."

Wasson said he believes that is the real story of the Miriamich fire, that of a community of people who faced tremendous odds and overcame them to become stronger and to build a vibrant, successful community.

Great Saint John Fire
(Black Wednesday)

June 20, 1877
Saint John, New Brunswick

"YESTERDAY WAS THE MOST CALAMITOUS day ever known in the annals of Saint John," was how the *Daily Telegraph* began its story the day following the deadly blaze.

The fire broke out on June 20, 1877. At the time, Saint John was one of the foremost port cities in the world, with a rich and affluent social elite class attached to the merchantry carried out from the city's wharves. Preceding the fire, it had not rained in three weeks, and the thermometer was registering around 25° C. A mid-morning breeze that soon became a brisk wind was at first perceived as a relief by the area's residents.

Soon, however, that breeze would become the enemy.

The whole conflagration began when an old barn storing hay caught fire near York Point Slip. As terrible fortune would have it, a brand new pumper engine was located in a fire station near the county courthouse, little more than a kilometre away from the flashpoint of the blaze, but, although the pumper was in fine working order, the team of horses needed to haul it was nowhere to be found. It seems that the horses and—although no one knew it at the time—much of the town were victims of a frugal decision at city hall to cut costs. Now the horses did exist, but it seems they were being shared with the public works department of the day—at the time the fire broke out, the horses were off doing hauling for a road construction project. By the time the horses were retrieved, several additional buildings had caught fire, and the situation had gone from manageable to desperate.

As the fire raged on, a total of 18 people lost their lives in the city of 50,000, and more than 1600 homes were destroyed in a span of about nine hours; 13,000 people were left homeless. The day would forever be recalled in Saint John as "Black Wednesday." As with many fires, the exact cause of the blaze was never determined, but there was speculation that an errant spark from a nearby mill may have been caught on the breeze and tossed onto the dry roof of the hay barn.

"The blaze was so huge, the light of its flames could be seen in the evening from Fredericton, more than 100 kilometres away," Mac Trueman, a retired reporter with the *Telegraph-Journal* in Saint John wrote on the 125th anniversary of the fire. "Within nine hours, it had reduced Saint John's downtown and south end to an unbroken landscape of smouldering ruins covering nearly a square kilometre from Saint John Harbour to Courtenay Bay."

"The fire obliterated most public buildings and businesses, including the post office, city hall, customs house, five banks, 14 hotels and 14 churches, as well as theatres and schools," Trueman went on. "The 1500 commercial and industrial buildings that were razed included 10 retail grocers, 116 liquor dealers, 93 commission merchants, 80 law offices, 55 boarding houses, 55 shoemakers, 36 tailors, 32 flour dealers, 29 insurance agents, 29 clothing stores and 22 dry goods establishments." Only about a quarter of the total damage, which was estimated at $27 million in 1877 dollars, was recovered from insurance settlements, he noted.

According to the *Daily Telegraph*, "Both sides of [Union] street were soon in the grasp of the devouring element, and the men [firefighters] lingered so long in their struggle to save the buildings that at last they were obliged to drop their branch pipes and run up the street, after which they dragged the hose after them."

In his *History of the Great Fire in Saint John, June 20 & 21, 1877*, Russell H. Conwell wrote, "So hot became the gusts, and so full of sparks was the air everywhere in the path of the tempest, that bundles of goods tossed from second-storey windows were on fire before they reached the hands of those who caught them in the yard below."

And, as Trueman commented in his anniversary article, "A thousand cast-outs sat with their remaining possessions at Queen Square, watching their homes burn, while looters circled around the square like vultures."

The *Daily Telegraph* further relayed the tragedy of the situation with these words:

> *"It was heart rending to witness sick, infirm and aged persons being dragged through the streets in search of a place of safety, which it was very difficult to find.*
>
> *"Women and children wept freely, and even full grown men could not restrain their emotions.*
>
> *"Streams of blood, the results of injuries, marked the faces of several men, and others had received bruises and [were] maimed in various ways.*
>
> *"Many men and women might be seen utterly exhausted, with the fatigue and the heat which becomes insufferable, dragging bedding, pieces of furniture and other articles through the streets, a vain task in many cases, as the new places of refuge sought out often proved as unsafe as those that were deserted."*

As Trueman recounts, "the *Telegraph* was one of nine newspapers whose offices were destroyed in the fire.

Both it and the *Globe* got editions on the street the next day by using borrowed printing houses."

"Clerks and employers," he went on to explain, "worked with hoses and buckets to fight against the fire on every roof on King Street, with little effect. In the South End, one man doused sparks with a water pitcher as they landed on his roof. He managed to keep his house standing for more than an hour before the fire went out of his control. He threw the pitcher down on the ledge of his chimney and fled for his life."

"The next day," wrote Gordon Shorter, then director of fire research for the National Research Council of Canada, in his 1967 report of the fire, "when people walked over the heap of ashes that once had been a household, they saw the old pitcher, standing on the ledge of the chimney."

Trueman noted that several accounts have been written of how James Allison's heroic effort stopped the fire from travelling up the north side of King Street. "Mr. Allison had his staff at Manchester Robertson spread hundreds of yards of carpeting and other heavy fabric across the roof of this dry goods store, soaking the material down with buckets of water before the fire got there," he noted. He went on to comment that although George Stewart, in his *The Story of the Great Fire in Saint John, N.B. June 20, 1877,* also lauded Mr. Allison's store as "the building which prevented the fire from extending up King Street," and that Mr. Shorter concurred, the *Globe* observed on June 24, 1877, that the fire had halted two buildings before the shop in question.

Among the King Street buildings to escape the flames was the famed Saint John City Market. Then, it was only about a year old; today, it is a historic landmark.

Describing the danger to the ships in port, Trueman wrote, "The middle of Saint John Harbour was a tangle of masts and yardarms of the square riggers that were hurriedly towed there from the piers and anchored. But with the tide out, the coastal schooners at Market Slip were stuck on the harbour bottom as if on flypaper. Their crews threw buckets of water on their vessels from stem to stern and waited in horror to see if the tide or the fire would get to them first. a total of 15 schooners burned at their moorings."

Trueman also observed that although the Bank of New Brunswick burned down, "its underground vault and the treasure with which it was hurriedly stuffed were undamaged."

In attesting to the importance of this vault and its contents, Trueman quoted a researcher as saying, "Without this building, there wouldn't have been any rebuilding of Saint John, because people wouldn't have had the money to do it."

Financial assistance to help the victims began to roll in from the United States and farther afield. "The City of Boston, which had suffered its own conflagration in 1873, sent $6200 to Saint John," noted Trueman. "More than $20,000 came in from Chicago, which had seen its big fire in 1871. Bangor [in Maine] sent $7000; the schoolchildren of Buffalo raised $1000; Charlottetown $5000, Fredericton $8000; Glasgow, Scotland, $14,600, among an endless list of contributors."

"Within a week of the fire," Trueman wrote, "the army that came to enforce martial law in Saint John found itself sharing its King Square encampment with a shanty town of businesses that refused to die.

"Much of the mercantile area along Prince William and King Street was under reconstruction within a year of the fire, under the direction of the same architects who rebuilt fire-ravaged Boston, and even statelier new mansions began to appear on Germain Street. Families that fled economic depression in the wake of the fire were now coming back to take part in the building boom," he continued.

"A few overgrown foundations, overlooked in the reconstruction, could still be found as late as 1957. In 1964, a construction project on Water Street unearthed a safe believed to have been buried during the Great Fire. It was empty, except for a key and some ashes," noted Trueman.

He went on to describe how, "In 1988, renovations of a turn-of-the-century Wentworth Street home uncovered a note left inside the wall by a disgruntled construction worker named John Edwards. It read: 'Came to this damned hole to get 1.50 cents [actually $1.50] per day. May the devil burn the damned town down again.'"

In 1982, the city of Saint John designated a 20-block uptown region as the Trinity Royal Heritage Preservation Area; it contains some 800 turn-of-the-century (post-fire) buildings. Nine years later, the National Historic Sites and Monuments Board declared it to be a national historic area.

"In an era when this city was a major world seaport and trade centre, the fourth largest shipbuilding centre in the world and one of the most prosperous cities in North America, wealthy merchants here competed against each other to create the most opulent homes and businesses, as the city rebuilt from the Great Fire of 1877," observed Trueman. And, according to local heritage planner Jim Bezanson, that's why uptown Saint John has the "largest and richest collection of turn-of-the-century architecture in all of Canada."

Great Commercial Street Fire

January 12, 1899
Bridgewater, Nova Scotia

ONE DAY AFTER THE JUBILANT Bridgewater band had ushered in the annual opening of the Exhibition Rink, the early morning hours of January 12, 1899, saw Bridgewater's 19th-century ascendancy brought to a screeching halt.

Officially, a Mrs. Carter who lived near the corner of Morgan and Commercial streets first spotted the blaze shortly after 3:00 AM. According to local historical records, the elderly woman shuffled to the window to see what the fuss was. Immediately, she spotted an orange hue emanating from T.B. Simonson's general store in the bottom level of the music hall and quickly realized that something was desperately wrong. As the unusual light came into focus for Mrs. Carter and the other onlookers, they managed to shake off the grogginess of the early hour and, moving as quickly as possible, spread the word from house to house—Bridgewater's beloved cultural centre, the Bridgewater Music Hall—was ablaze.

The community's fire engine was called, its crew assembling as fast as possible, but Bridgewater's waterfront was a collection of wooden buildings, built in close proximity and in places interconnecting. By the time the fire brigade was on the scene, the music hall building and several other neighbouring structures were already fully engulfed by flames. A strong winter's wind blowing out of the northwest helped to fan the fire as it jumped steadily from one building to the next.

Any progress the fire brigade attempted to make was disrupted by Mother Nature—the cold made spraying difficult, and any water lying in long, straight sections of hose froze frequently, stalling efforts to control the beast that would become known to locals as the Great Commercial Street Fire. As the inferno moved relentlessly amid the buildings along the west side of Commercial Street, farthest from the river, the flames ignited a store of gunpowder in a hardware store. The resulting explosion tossed burning debris in all directions; some of it flew across Commercial Street into the Patillo Brothers' store, where a second epicentre was ignited.

In the hours that followed, both sides of Commercial Street, the heart of Bridgewater's impressive service-based economy, were razed to the ground. The best efforts of the townsfolk, and the arrival of a supporting fire engine from nearby Lunenburg, helped to control the fire as it roared for more than a kilometre along the length of Commercial Street, from the music hall as far as the Liverpool Road. But, by the time the sun dawned over Bridgewater on the morning of January 12, 1899, the only proof that the smouldering rubble along the LaHave River had been an intricate complex of businesses the night before could be found in photographs taken by H.O. Dodge from the east bank of the LaHave River as the calamity took place.

In total, 54 buildings were destroyed, causing hundreds of thousands of dollars in damage. Newspapers, locally and beyond, reverberated with word of Bridgewater's decimation. The *Acadian Recorder* and *Halifax Herald* each sent reporters to the community to give an account of the losses. In Bridgewater, the offices of the *Bridgewater Bulletin* and the *LaHave Gazette* were swallowed by the fire. The *Bulletin* would take one week before it began printing a miniature, four-page "Fire Edition" of its weekly standard, with the words, "We are little, but we'll grow," in bold text beneath the masthead. The *Gazette* issued one edition the week following the fire but then elected to wait until its office was completely operational again, approximately one month later, before publishing its second weekly following the devastation of the community's riverfront.

Remarkably, despite the extent of the destruction, the Great Commercial Street Fire claimed no residential houses and only one life. Even the death of Henry C. Barnaby, a local merchant and valued community contributor, was not directly related to the blaze itself but to the ruckus that ensued as townspeople rushed to watch the fire cut its destructive path. Mr. Barnaby, who was viewing the fire, was accidentally run down by a team of horses. It was believed Barnaby had suffered severe head trauma, as he slipped in and out of delirium for 10 days before succumbing to his injuries.

But, reflecting the nature of a resourceful community, the spirit of the people of Bridgewater was not obliterated by the fire. In the days following the blaze, as smoke still wafted from many charred buildings, a relief committee was organized by the citizens of Bridgewater to assist those stricken by the destruction. The *Bulletin* made note of the almost ebullient way in which the townsfolk did their best to go about business as usual, despite the destruction that had befallen their beloved hub, with editor Cragg writing: "Most of our homes have escaped destruction. It is wonderful to note the cheerful way in which our people...are looking misfortune squarely in the face. The noise of the hammer and saw are heard way into the night."

And it would seem that most people, particularly the afflicted merchants and businessmen, did their best to ensure the community did not lapse into the despair that had gripped many other similar towns affected by fire. In many cases, Bridgewater's merchants set up temporary shacks along what remained of Commercial Street to sell what they could and to collect on as many debts as possible. Other, more fortunate organizations and agencies were permitted to establish temporary headquarters at the community's courthouse. The multi-level facility became a hive of business activity, serving as a temporary home for W.E. Marshall (the registrar of deeds), a number of barristers (including the firm Wade & Paton), bank brokers, the post office, the Western Union Telegraph Company and the Bridgewater Power Company. No local business better exemplified both the extent of the utter destruction felt in Bridgewater's commercial district and, at the same time, sheer defiance against such trauma, than the *Bulletin* itself. The paper advised its patrons in print on January 24, less than two weeks after the Commercial Street fire, that "The *Bulletin* office is on the corner of Commercial and Dufferin Streets (if anybody knows where that is), and is ready and willing for business."

One of the other daunting tasks that faced the merchants of Bridgewater following the fire was assessing their losses for insurance purposes. Merchants set to work almost immediately filling out forms and filing claims to recoup some of the losses caused by the fire. Upon a thorough examination by the insurance adjustors dispatched, one of the lead adjustors, C.E.L. Jarvis, concluded that in total the community's losses were estimated at $245,000. (Using the Consumer Price Index conversion formula developed by Robert Sahr at Oregon State University, that's almost $5.5 million in 2007 Canadian money). Jarvis and his team ultimately awarded just over $120,000 total in compensation to the merchants of Bridgewater, from more than 20 different insurance carriers, underscoring that many citizens of Bridgewater were prepared for the possibility of a disaster caused by fire. The biggest payout came from Québec Insurance, which had to compensate its clients with more than $24,600.

In his report, Jarvis also made a series of recommendations to the town's officials designed to keep insurance
rates down and to ensure that such a catastrophe could
be avoided in the future. Among the suggestions, Jarvis
urged Bridgewater to take the steps necessary to install
a community-owned waterworks system, noting that
one with large mains for greater capacity could encour-
age steam-driven business enterprises to court the community. Jarvis also advocated height restrictions for
buildings, the prohibition of wooden rooftop shingles
and the construction of brick buildings once the rebuilding of Commercial Street hit full stride.

No definitive cause was ever found for the Great
Commercial Street Fire. However, the point of origin
was found to be T.B. Simonson's store, which was
located just below the music hall, but there was little
evidence to indicate the source of the catastrophe. In all
likelihood, investigators concluded, a stray spark from
a stove not quite fully extinguished the evening before
had ignited the blaze. In any event, the fire had important long-term implications in Bridgewater, in addition
to the short-term damage to the business district.

Three weeks after the blaze, on February 4, 1899, residents voted to incorporate Bridgewater. The debate over
whether or not the community ought to become a town
had been raging for several years. The Great Commercial
Street Fire of 1899 had a tremendous impact on the
development of Bridgewater, Nova Scotia. Not only was
the business district forced to redesign itself, thus creating a safer, more adaptable working environment in the
long term, but it's even possible that without the blaze
the community might have sidestepped the issue of
incorporation altogether.

Halifax Explosion

December 6, 1917
Halifax, Nova Scotia

THURSDAY, DECEMBER 6, 1917, was a sunny but cold winter day, the kind that would make a person hasten his or her step as the snow crunched underfoot. With World War I underway, the port city of Halifax, Nova Scotia, was a busy place, with ships coming and going as they transported their cargos of troops, relief supplies and munitions in support of the war effort overseas.

At approximately 8:00 AM, the *Imo*, a Norwegian ship, headed up Bedford Basin en route to New York to pick up relief supplies to deliver to Belgium. And it was about that same time that the *Mont-Blanc*, a French supply ship, steamed into Halifax Harbour to meet a convoy that would accompany her across the treacherous Atlantic Ocean. According to historical data, the *Mont-Blanc* was laden with explosives: "35 tons of benzol, 300 rounds of ammunition, 10 tons of gun cotton, 2300 tons of picric acid (used in explosives) and 400,000 pounds [180,000 kilograms] of TNT." The *Imo* was a much faster and more massive ship than the *Mont-Blanc*, and it would later be revealed that she was travelling too fast and in the wrong channel as she headed quickly into the Narrows. It was in the Narrows that the *Mont-Blanc* first spotted the *Imo*, moving quickly in its directions and in its channel.

The *Mont-Blanc* signalled that she was in the correct channel, but the *Imo* replied that she was not changing course. (Had the *Mont-Blanc* been flying the requisite red flag to indicate her deadly cargo, one might hope that the captain of the *Imo* would have reacted more prudently, but the *Mont-Blanc* had wanted to avoid being targeted by the Germans.) The *Mont-Blanc,* expecting the *Imo* to swing towards the Halifax side of the harbour, signalled that she was intending to pass on the starboard (right) side. By this time, the *Mont-Blanc* was precariously close to Dartmouth and had slowed to a snail's pace. However, instead of turning towards Halifax, as the *Mont-Blanc* had anticipated, the *Imo* maintained its course. This left the master of the *Mont-Blanc* with only one apparent course of action, and that was to swing to port (left), in the direction of Halifax, a move that would take her directly across the bow of the *Imo,* thus allowing her to pass on the starboard side.

This strategy might have worked had the *Imo* not simultaneously reversed her propeller. A collision ensued as the *Imo's* bow swung to starboard, striking the *Mont-Blanc.* The colliding ship missed the TNT cargo, but it did strike the picric acid, which was stored underneath the drums of benzol. The impact of the two ships cut a gaping hole in the *Mont-Blanc*, creating sparks in the process.

Amid the resulting blaze, the crew of the *Mont-Blanc,* aware of their deadly cargo, quickly abandoned ship, taking to the lifeboats or diving into the water. The deserted, flaming *Mont-Blanc,* propelled by the impact of the *Imo,* was now headed directly towards the port city of Halifax. It drifted until it rested against Pier 6, which was located in the Richmond district of the busy industrial North End of Halifax. The thrilling spectacle drew crowds of spectators, unaware of the danger. Although sailors of the *Mont-Blanc* who reached shore screamed out warnings, the locals failed to react, because they did not understand French. It was now just after 9:00 AM on that fateful morning.

Twenty minutes following the collision, the *Mont-Blanc* violently exploded, resulting in the largest human-caused

The Norwegian steamship *Imo,* one of two boats that collided in Halifax Harbour on December 16, 1917. Following the collision, the *Imo* ran aground on the Dartmouth shore.

❦

explosion ever (until the invention of nuclear weapons) and sending a powerful shock wave out in all directions for kilometres. Then, for some 10 minutes, a thick black carbon coating fell from the sky. The human and monetary cost was tremendous. More than 1900 people died immediately, and an additional 100 or so died of their injuries over the following months. It was estimated that the explosion injured a further 9000 people, and approximately 130 hectares—almost the entire North End of Halifax—were devastated by the blast and the ensuing tsunami. The resulting fires eventually consumed most of the structures in the vicinity that had been left standing after the explosion.

As for the *Mont-Blanc*, the 8800 cubic metre ship was totally destroyed, her shattered remains flung far and wide for several kilometres in all directions. According to accounts of the explosions, the barrel of one cannon crashed to earth some 5.5 kilometres away, and a chunk of her anchor shank, weighing over 500 kilograms, was found 3 kilometres in the reverse direction. The shock wave had tremendous force, shattering windows up to 80 kilometres away. Reports from as far away as Sydney, Cape Breton—435 kilometres from Halifax—revealed the blast was felt even at that great a distance.

The relief efforts began within hours, but, as one might expect, the hospitals were overwhelmed. And, to make matters worse, a terrible winter blizzard struck the city the following day, depositing more than 40 centimetres of snow on the ruins of the once-bustling city and its human sufferers.

In time, however, the city was rebuilt. Today, only a few survivors of the infamous Halifax Explosion are still alive to tell their tragic stories. Catherine Gertrude (Gert) Roy was born in 1896 in Halifax. She moved to Liverpool, Nova Scotia, in 1917 following the explosion. She witnessed the catastrophe and lived to tell about it. "I remember that was a hectic, frightening time. It was a bad day for the entire city; many people died, and many more were hurt really bad," Gert recalled years after the disaster:

> "I can say without hesitation that it was the most horrible day of my life. It was like the entire world stood still for us. Everyone thought the Germans were bombing us. After all, we were still in the middle of the First World War. I remember hearing once how someone suggested that a German warship had been anchored just off the coast and fired a bomb at us, but that story turned out to be false. But it was terrible just the same.

As seen from a distance of 20 kilometres, a column of thick, dark smoke rises from the Halifax Explosion. This image is believed to be the only photograph of the blast itself.

I remember when the explosion happened, all I heard was a terrible crash, or boom, sort of like thunder, but three times louder than thunder... a lot louder. Then that was immediately followed by the sounds of breaking windows and doors slamming and wood twisting and buildings crashing down around us, and people screaming and crying out for help. It was the worst thing anyone could ever image. Anyone who survived those first few minutes was lucky to be alive."

Or maybe not.

Married for only a few months at the time of the explosion, the young woman and her husband, Ralph, had been living in Black Court in the North End of Halifax, about 2.5 kilometres from the explosion site. Stating that she can remember the event just as if it had happened only yesterday, Gert said, "The explosion was so strong that it shook the whole city, and they say they felt it way down here in Liverpool, so you can imagine how it felt in the city."

She continued, "It was just terrible. So many people died or were injured that day. I had a sister who lost an eye in the explosion, but my family were pretty lucky that more didn't happen to them. Some families were not as lucky. Entire families were wiped out. That's a sad thing to think about. In just a matter of minutes, entire families were destroyed...Mothers, fathers, sons and daughters—babies and children—were all gone. How does anyone recover from that?"

As in the case of Gert's sister, eye injuries were among the most common malady reported from the explosion. Because many Halifax residents had rushed to their windows to see the burning ship just prior to the blast, when the explosion occurred, hundreds of people were sprayed with shards of glass from the shattering windows. Gert said she could remember hearing stories of people removing glass from under their skin even years after that dreadful day.

It was the memories of death and human suffering that remained with Gert her entire life, in vivid detail, through the years. "The injured children are what I remember the most," she added. "And they all seemed so lost. There were hundreds of them wandering aimlessly around the ruins, crying and looking for their mommies and daddies, but, for many of them, their parents were never found, as their families were gone."

Records of the time show that police tried to relocate those lost children with their families, but many were found to have become orphans, yet another profound impact of the catastrophe.

But, despite their hardships, at least these children were alive. Many were not. Gert described how on the days following the explosion she saw "little white caskets lined up row upon row on the city streets holding the bodies of the hundreds of children that had been killed in the explosions or later succumbed to their injuries or to the cold." Schools and other buildings became make-shift morgues as officials sought to find places to store the bodies until they could be identified by families or later disposed of.

Death had become commonplace in the shattered city. Corpses, body parts, dead horses and dogs were everywhere, and Gert recalls all the terrible smells. "I remember on the north side there used to be an onion factory and a stable located almost next to each other. As the factory and stables burned, you could smell an odour similar to that of beef and onions in the air," she recalled, adding, "I couldn't eat beef and onions for the longest while after that. It made me ill."

The smells, she said, stayed with her for a long time, especially the stench of burning human flesh. "It's just a terrible thing. It actually gets in and burns your nose. I remember at times smelling this sickly, sweet smell in the air, and I had no idea what it was. "Later" Gert explained, "I found out that it was the smell of human flesh being consumed by the fires that burned uncontrollably for days."

Trying to describe the scene after the explosion, Gert said it was even worse than anyone can imagine. "Total, absolute destruction," is how she summed it up. "The entire North End of the city was wiped out. Streets were gone. Buildings were levelled. People were killed and injured and bleeding and in need of medical help which couldn't keep up...It was total hell. That's really the best way I can think of to describe it."

Of the next day's blizzard, Gert recalled, "It was the biggest snowstorm you could imagine, and there wasn't a window left in the whole city. It was cold, very cold, which made the suffering even worse. I remember we faced some very tough times following the explosion. You just can't even begin to imagine what that was like. We all felt so helpless and lost."

For the survivors of the explosion, Gert said that trying to pull their lives back together was extremely difficult because they just could not forget about the many people who had been killed or injured and all those who lost family members. But, she noted, time passes, and the scars do eventually heal. "I'll never ever be able to forget the tragedy of the Halifax Explosion. It's impossible to forget something that killed and injured so many people. You just can't do it, but you find a way to go on. You might try to forget, but pictures like those get in your head, and they're buried there forever," she finished.

Thankfully, the thousands of well-disciplined troops and naval resources helped rescue efforts begin quickly in the aftermath of the explosion. Local officials promptly coordinated volunteer help, and the Halifax Relief Committee had been organized before sunset. Reinforcements from throughout the region poured in to help. Although every building still standing—and even the ships in the vicinity—was pressed into service to shelter the wounded and homeless, some of these people still had to be put on a train to be looked after in other communities.

Thanks to ships' radio, Boston, Massachusetts, received news of the disaster within hours of the event. Wasting no time, the city sent off their first trainload of supplies that night along with medical personnel and members of the Public Safety Committee. Assistance continued to arrive from the rest of Canada and from around the world, but the quick generosity of Massachusetts was especially touching to the city's stricken citizens. As a token of their gratitude, each Christmas since 1971, the people of Nova Scotia supply the huge Christmas tree that graces Boston Common.

When final tallies of the explosion's impact were made, records show that a total of 1630 homes were entirely destroyed and a further 12,000 houses were damaged, leaving 6000 people seeking shelter. The force of the blast had shattered almost all the windows in both Halifax and Dartmouth.

Of the over 1900 dead, about 250 bodies were never identified; conversely, many victims could not be found. Hospitals and doctors in private practice together treated between 4000 and 5000 injured; they amputated 25 limbs and removed over 250 injured eyes, leaving 37 unfortunate souls totally blind.

Following the explosion, soldiers were called in to locate and help survivors. The death toll rose to just over 1900 in the wake of the blast. About 250 bodies were never identified; many victims were never found.

~∞C∞

When word got around as to the cause of the disaster, the public was furious and demanded answers. Within a week of the explosion, an official inquiry was launched. On February 4, 1918, the *Mont-Blanc* was found to be solely at fault. The captain of the *Mont-Blanc* and its local pilot were charged with manslaughter as was the chief examining officer of Halifax Harbour. The latter was acquitted, and charges were dropped against the other two, because it was determined that gross negligence could not be proven. After the matter went back and forth in the courts for a time, eventually an appeal to the Supreme Court of Canada found both ships equally responsible; this decision was affirmed by the Judicial Committee of the Privy Council in Britain, the highest court of appeal for Canadians at that time.

When all was said and done, no one was ever punished for the Halifax Explosion.

Recognizing how their damaged city could be improved, Haligonians rebuilt carefully to a very high standard—the Hydrostone development is a prime example. In addition, they improved the quantity and quality of the healthcare facilities and enhanced the social welfare network. Finally, they brought in more stringent harbour regulations to minimize the chance of future marine mishaps.

Of the gravestones, artifacts and monuments throughout Halifax and Dartmouth that serve as reminders of the explosion, Fort Needham's Memorial Bell Tower is especially noteworthy. Of its 14 bells, 10 originally hung in the United Memorial Church, which replaced two churches destroyed in the Halifax Explosion. Back in 1920, Barbara Orr, who as a teenager had lost her entire family—mother, father and two brothers and three sisters—in the disaster, had donated them to the church. Eventually, the church tower could no longer support them, and they were installed in the memorial tower in 1985. Every December 6 at 9:00 AM, the bells ring out through the North End and across the water to Dartmouth as part of a service held in memory of the victims of the Halifax Explosion.

It may be interesting to note that the Halifax Explosion has been the fodder of conspiracy theorists who have attempted to pin a German connection on this devastating World War I explosion. From the moment the blast happened, because of the paranoia of wartime, there were attempts to link the explosion to German subterfuge. This is quite understandable given that the city had an antisubmarine net at the mouth of its harbour that was closed each night to thwart any would-be lurking German U-boats.

Such hysteria in a time of war can be expected to a certain degree. But the weird thing about Halifax is that the suspicion of a German connection has never completely died off completely. In 1989, Janet Kitz wrote a book about the explosion in which she interviewed survivors who were still convinced that there must have been some sort of German plot. The nearly century-old furore over German involvement was brought to a new generation in the CBC's production of *Shattered City,* in which the writers took the creative liberty of injecting German spies into the plot. Historians have roundly rejected this notion time and again, and yet here it is, being presented on national television to an audience who may be learning for the first time about the story of the Halifax Explosion.

But, for the people who lived through the nightmare, the real story of the Halifax Explosion is one of survival. It's a story of the human will to overcome seemingly insurmountable odds and to rise above difficult challenges. It's a story of people reaching out to help people in their time of need. It is the true story of perseverance and of beating the odds. Amid all the death and destruction, the suffering and sorrow, there was also inspiration and hope. For people such as Gert Roy, that's the real story.

St. John's Knights of Columbus Hall Fire

December 12, 1942
St. John's, Newfoundland

THE STORY HIT THE FRONT PAGE of the St. John's *Evening Telegram* on December 14, 1942, two days after the event. It told of death and destruction unlike anything the people of this small Newfoundland city had seen before, or since.

About 500 people were having a good time on a blustery cold Saturday night at the Knights of Columbus Leave Centre on Harvey Road in St. John's, and people throughout the city were listening along to a live radio broadcast from the site. Suddenly, just after 11:00 PM, the music came to an abrupt stop.

Shouts of "Fire! Fire!" suddenly rang through the building, and panic gripped the air. The fear was palpable. People tried to escape the inferno, but to no avail because many of the exits and all the windows were covered over as part of wartime blackout regulations. Within five minutes, anybody still left inside the flimsy building was dead—burned alive or quickly overcome by smoke and gases from the inferno. A total of 99 deaths occurred, along with over 100 injuries. The fire station was less than a kilometre away, but that didn't matter because the hall went up like a tinderbox. There was little chance of rescue.

When the blaze happened, Newfoundland was not yet a part of Canada, so it is only since 1949 that the Knights of Columbus Hall blaze has ranked among the deadliest structure fires in Canadian history.

According to Robert Parsons, who specializes in the history of Newfoundland's small fishing communities along the province's south coast, among the victims was Private Bertram Baker, a member of the Newfoundland Regiment. He was one of the many servicemen in the hall attending the dance that night when the fire struck. He perished in the blaze, and his name can now be found inscribed on a bronze plaque at Grand Bank Memorial Library. Three other individuals from the community of Grand Bank perished in the fire: Private George Lambert and civilians Emma Hickman and Rose Thorne also died in that night's mayhem.

Parsons, who wrote about the stories of Newfoundland in his book *Born Down by the Water,* says the St. John's fire was a disaster of unequalled proportions, even by today's standards:

> *"It left a legacy of death and destruction, along with a mystery that has not been solved to this very day. There was widespread speculation about the cause of the fire, including that it was arson or some other form sabotage, but nothing was ever proven. Even an inquiry that followed the fire failed to produce any clear evidence that the blaze had been deliberately set. To this day, people will say the fire was set by a spy working against the Allies during the war, but that theory has never been backed up by any proof."*

Of the indoor conflagrations in the history of Canadian disasters, this Knights of Columbus Hall Fire was the quickest and most deadly. Previously, that unwanted title had been held by the tragic January 9, 1927, fire in the Laurier Palace Movie Theatre in Montréal; although it was quickly extinguished, 76 children were crushed or suffocated while trying to escape in the ensuing panic.

The St. John's fire was devastating, and many people in the community believed the blaze was almost certainly lit by an enemy agent, who, according to local legend, "cunningly… used rolls of toilet paper as his torch." However, as Parsons points out, these types of stories often follow such a tragedy. It is true that the city may have been a target for spies working in the war effort, Parsons concedes. "But was a spy responsible for this deadly fire? I don't know…It seems the cause will remain a mystery forever," Parsons admits.

During this time in its history, because of its location, the port city of St. John's was a convenient place for Allied convoys to gather before making the voyage across the Atlantic. Enemy agents were well aware of the opportunities to be found here, and they did their best to infiltrate the bustling, bursting town and gather what intelligence they could. Therefore, it is not surprising that rumours of subterfuge and sabotage by a German agent were rampant in the community for some time after the December 12 fire, but such innuendo was never conclusively proven. Today, the cause for one of Canada's deadliest structure fires in history remains a mystery, buried in the dust of time.

Nova Scotia's Mining Disasters

1800s and 1900s
Various Locations

- Drummond Colliery Disaster, Westville, 1873 (60–70 deaths)
- Ford Pit Explosion, Stellarton, 1880 (50 deaths)
- Springhill Mine Disaster, 1891 (125 deaths)
- Cape Breton Gas Explosion, Florence, 1911 (14 deaths)
- Dominion No. 12 Colliery Explosion, New Waterford, 1917 (65 deaths)
- Albion Mine Explosion, Stellarton, 1918 (88 deaths)
- Sydney Mines, cable break in mine shaft, 1938 (20 deaths)
- Springhill Explosion, 1956 (39 deaths)
- Springhill Bump, 1958 (74 or 75 deaths)
- Westray Coal Mine Explosion, Plymouth, 1992 (26 deaths)

–Primarily from the Government of Nova Scotia Archives & Records website

COAL MINING IS INHERENTLY LINKED to Cape Breton Island, much in the same way that the isle itself is inextricably linked to the North Atlantic. Mining began on the island almost immediately after permanent European colonists arrived. Initially, coal was taken from seams that had naturally ripped through the surface, making it easily accessible. In 1720, Cape Breton's first mine was opened at Cow Bay, which is known today as the community of Port Morien.

Over the next 190 years, the natural fuel source blossomed as an integral part of Cape Breton's economic health.

By the early 20th century, the Sydney region was one of Canada's booming industrial centres. With a population that ranked as the 21st largest in the country, much of the community's growth had been spurred on by the emergence of the coal industry, led by the behemoth Dominion Coal Company (DCC). According to the Cape Breton Miners Museum, by 1912, the DCC had 16 collieries (coal mines) operational and was responsible for nearly half of the entire country's coal production. Employment opportunities were abundant, and the region attracted many immigrants from across the Atlantic, whereas others crossed the Gulf of St. Lawrence from Newfoundland.

The reward for taking to the mines was high for miners and their families, but the risk was equally high. Whether it was a freak accident involving a wild rail car or a catastrophic explosion that ripped a mine's inner labyrinth to shreds, there were always plenty of perils of which to be wary.

By its very nature, the mining industry, particularly the mining of coal, is ripe for tragedy. The combination of long underground tunnels, fragile rock, dangerous dust and explosives, along with ventilation systems that sometimes fail, is a recipe for trouble. Although significant disasters have happened in coal mines in various parts of Canada, a particularly long list of tragedies has occurred in Nova Scotia.

❧◆❧

Nova Scotia's first large mining catastrophe, the Drummond Colliery Disaster of May 13, 1873, was also, according to *The Canadian Encyclopedia Historica*, the first such accident recorded in Canada. Beginning in 1865, several collieries (coal mines) had set up in the Westville area to mine a recently discovered seam of the Pictou Coalfield. The approximately 350 men and boys who worked the Drummond used both gunpowder and pickaxes to break off chunks of the valuable black rock for their employer.

On that unfortunate May day, the routine use of a gunpowder charge to mine the uppermost coalface caused flammable gas to escape, and a fire broke out. As smoke filled the mine, the ventilation system failed, and more gas seeped into the shaft. Realizing that the fire could not be controlled, the mine manager ordered the men to evacuate, but the order came too late. The ensuing explosion killed or injured the majority of the miners. Just as rescue attempts began, a second explosion rocked the mine, killing one rescuer outright and almost killing two others.

Witnesses reported seeing 1400-foot (425-metre) flames shooting up from the mine. Meanwhile, secondary shafts violently expelled rocks, wooden beams and equipment up to 400 metres away.

Some 60 men died, and they left behind 31 widows and 80 fatherless children. Because the mine was for a time sealed to keep oxygen from feeding the flames, it took two years before all the bodies had been recovered.

Another terrible incident occurred on January 3, 1911. A total of 14 miners perished in a gas explosion at the No. 3 Colliery at Florence. It was an accident that proved devastating for the mining community in Cape Breton County and also for families in Newfoundland, from whence many of the miners had come.

Another of the province's significant mining disasters, the worst in Cape Breton at the time, occurred at the No. 12 Colliery in New Waterford in 1917.

The first coal mining near the town of New Waterford (formerly Barrachois), Cape Breton, occurred at Lingan as early as 1854, and further operations began 11 years later at Low Point. In 1907, the huge Dominion Coal Company moved into the area.

Over the next decade, a total of 11 coal pits came into production as mining became the region's driving economic industry. However, the dangers of coal mining are well chronicled in the annals of Nova Scotian history.

On July 25, 1917, at around 7:00 AM, some 270 men commenced work in the Dominion No. 12 Colliery.

At 7:30 AM, a powerful blast occurred about seven levels down and 640 metres from the entrance, instantly killing over 60 men and boys between the ages of 14 and 65.

When they went down to offer assistance to the miners, two 17-year-old workers who had been aboveground at the time also died. Another rescuer was more successful, managing nine trips to retrieve his fellow miners before he himself succumbed to the deadly gas. At least one young man spent three days underground before being rescued. Of the 65 men killed that day, 22 were Newfoundlanders.

⋘◆⋙

For coal miners, death is an all-too-immediate threat. Underground tragedies can come in the guise of dust explosions, fires, cave-ins or deadly gases. To stay alive, miners must keep alert at all times to avert hazards such as accidental drowning and mishaps with heavy machinery. Then, even if they beat the odds underground, there is still the lurking possibility of succumbing to a lung ailment such as silicosis or black lung. Over the course of its storied history, the province of Nova Scotia has experienced many calamitous mining accidents that have, collectively, left thousands dead and untold additional miners injured.

As of this writing, nearly 2600 of the countless workers who have died in the course of Nova Scotia's mining and quarrying operations over the last three centuries have been listed in a government-run searchable database, *Nova Scotia Mine Fatalities 1838–1992*. Giving the miners' names as well as the circumstances surrounding their deaths, the site serves as an online cenotaph honouring those who perished far beneath the earth's crust. This record of deaths suffered in the famed mines of Cape Breton stretches on for pages.

Springhill Mine Disaster
(The Explosion)

November 1, 1956
Springhill, Nova Scotia

SPRINGHILL, CUMBERLAND COUNTY, is located to the southeast of Amherst, Nova Scotia. According to the "Place-Names and Places of Nova Scotia" (PNPNS) series published by the Public Archives of Nova Scotia, Springhill got its name pretty much the way one would expect—the town is located on a hill that once contained many springs. Europeans began settling in the area as early the 1820s, with the first nearby schoolhouse being constructed in 1853 and the first church about a decade later.

According to PNPNS, the first person to discover coal in the Springhill area was a fellow named Lodovick Hunter. He was a member of one of the settlement's founding families, and his discovery took place in 1834, not long after the settlement had been founded.

Coal, one could say, has pretty much almost always been directly linked to Springhill's existence. Despite finding coal at such an early date and the fact that a mining contract and the rights to 160 acres (64.8 hectares) of land had been awarded to a company as early as the 1840s, it was not until the 1870s that large-scale coal-mining operations began in the community. But when the industry took off, the community grew with the mines. Railways were constructed to nearby centres such as Parrsboro in order to transport the coal. Springhill was formally incorporated as a town in 1889. But, as was often the case, coal mining was a dangerous mistress for the budding little industrial centre.

Surface buildings at No. 1 Slope of the Springhill Mine in 1897.

On February 21, 1891, just after noon, the first signifi-cant mining accident occurred with a major fire and explosions that claimed the lives of 125 individuals. A fire caused by a buildup of coal dust swept through the No. 1 and No. 2 collieries, which were connected by a tunnel more than 300 metres below the surface. All told, some 57 women were left widowed by the incident. An inquiry into the exact cause of the fire in an effort to discover what ignited the coal dust could not determine what had struck the first spark, although it was able to pinpoint the approximate location of the fire.

Such was life in a mining community. Things stum-bled onwards. In 1910, the old Cumberland Railway and

The 1894 "White Miner" monument in Springhill bears the names of those killed in the explosion of 1891. On the granite pedestal, which is 5 metres high, stands this figure, in white marble, of a coal miner with a pick and a safety lamp.

Coal Company was bought by the Dominion Coal Company, which eventually evolved into the Dominion Steel and Coal Corporation. The next major disaster would not happen for another 65 years.

❧◆❧

Ken Melanson remembers that November 1, 1956, dawned a beautiful sunny day. He also recalls that as he got ready for work in the mines that afternoon, his thoughts were elsewhere, thinking how nice it would have been to do anything else that would allow him to stay out of the mines that day, but that wasn't possible. So, resigned to his lot in life, the 19-year-old miner went about his routine just as he did every day.

Ken had started working in the Springhill coal mines at the age of 16 because, he says, when you lived in the Springhill area, that is what you did—you went down underground to make a living. As children, he and his friends went to school, but, when a boy turned 15 or 16, it was usually off to the mines for him.

"It was our way of life. I knew when I turned 16 that's what I would be doing," he continues, his voice remaining strong and proud:

> "It was a good, honest living... But it was a hard living. I followed my family into the mines. My father was a coal miner, my grandfather was a coal miner. It was a way of life, just like farming and fishing is a way of life in other communities. We did what we had to do, and, in those days, we were thankful that we had a place to go to work. Coal was the king in these parts, and anyone working in the mines made pretty good money. You earned it, mind you, but it was a pretty good living just the same. Some people went into lumbering in the woods, and a lot of the fellows went off and joined

the army, but, for anyone who stayed in Springhill, it
was the mines."

In those days, Ken explains, although the mining jobs were dangerous and hard, they also paid pretty well. "Or at least we thought we made pretty good wages compared to what other people were making," he notes.

In 1956, an average coal miner would have earned $10.12 per shift ($79.03 in 2007 money). When that rate is compared to the pay for other jobs in the area, Ken points out, it's easy to understand why so many men took the risks in the mines. "Working in the woods, for instance, earned you about $4.00 a shift. That was a pretty big difference, and, when you have a family to take care of, the men were willing to gamble. Coal miners were considered to be pretty well off" he explains, "but obviously we know the men were paid better than most men in other jobs because of the dangers associated with the work."

Whatever the money, however, Ken says that anyone going down into the mines still had to like the work, or at least accept it, or he would be miserable. "I liked the coal mines. The one thing about the mines for me, was that it was always the same down there underground. Nothing changed. For 12 months of the year, it was dark no matter the time of day, and the temperatures were always constant down there. It didn't matter if it was winter, spring, summer or fall—nothing changed down there for the miners. It didn't matter if it was sweltering hot or freezing cold on the surface, below the ground, we knew once we got down there, it would be just as it always was—cool, but not too cold. It was actually very comfortable," Ken affirms.

Thursday, November 1, 1956, was a normal working day for Ken. "I remember the day very well...Very, very well," he reminisces. "It was a bright, beautiful Indian summer day. The sun was out and it was very warm considering the time of year."

On that afternoon, Ken remembers his mother packing his lunch in the can he always took down into the mine with him. At this mine, the crews began their various shifts on Monday, and their rotation ended after the Thursday night shift. This was the final day of Ken's rotation in this set of shifts. After that, the following Monday, he would start the earlier shift. There were three shifts per day, and they usually worked eight to nine hours each shift. In the No. 4 mine, where Ken was working, the crews were hired on contract, which meant if they met their quota early, they could leave. Most of the time, though, they had to work seven or eight hours before they were finished.

Beyond the hours that were actually spent working in the mine, Ken says that travel time also had to be considered. "It took about an hour, from the time you left the surface, to get to your workplace. There and back, took about two hours, so you had to take that out of your 24 hours [in a day], but that was the routine."

On the way to the mine that day, Ken met up with two of his best friends, Floyd Beaton and Richard Ellis. Together, the trio went to the mine, which was owned by Dominion Steel and Coal. "I remember saying to the fellows how it was such a nice day," Ken recalls. "I said to them that it was too bad we have to work and that we just couldn't run off and find something to do outside. It was so warm that day that people were just going about in their shirtsleeves. That was pretty warm for November."

Upon changing out of their street clothes and into their mining coveralls, Ken and his two friends collected their buckets and put on their steel-toed boots to protect their feet from falling rocks. After donning their pit helmets, the men picked up their check numbers.

Every miner who went into the pits was assigned a number. That's how the company kept track of the men as they went down into the shafts. The next stop was the lamp cabin. In order to get their lamps, the men were required to turn over their check-number slips. When they came back up and turned in their lamps, they'd get their slips back. "If, after the shift ended and the men came up, they [the people in the lamp cabin] still had a check slip left, they knew they had a problem and that there was still a man down in the mines, " Ken elaborates. "It was a simple system, but it worked." Ken's number was 2238.

With his two friends, Ken went outside and waited under an apple tree for the trolleys to arrive from deep within the mine to bring up the men from the shift just ending and pick up the new crew; 125 others waited with them. Sadly, Ken points out, although he had no reason to suspect so at the time, it turned out to be the last time he would have with his friends.

At about 3:20 PM, the first of the two trolleys arrived to take the waiting men down into the dark, cool pits. Ken and his friends waited for the second car. Finally, at about 3:40 PM, they were on their way down to their workplace, approximately 1700 metres down the pit's west wall.

Arriving at his work site about 4:05 PM, Ken quickly went about his job, which was shovelling coal onto a conveyor belt that would take it to the trolley cars. "I liked to work and keep busy because it made the time go more quickly," he said. "I figured I had a job to do and got right at it."

He had been working, he estimated, for about an hour when he suddenly felt a strong gust of wind race down the shaft. The miners knew that at such a depth wind was unusual, but they had no idea what it meant.

Later, a Royal Commission would find that a trolley of coal had gone up a slope against the prevailing flow of air. As a result, coal dust had been blown back into the mine and created what amounted to an underground powder-keg just waiting to go off. The spark to ignite it was created when, just before reaching the surface, at least one of the empty trolley cars came loose and sped back down into the mine, derailing and careening into a 25,000-volt power line.

The explosion was instant. Sparks from the crash ignited the coal dust at the 1670-metre level. The flames caused an explosion so powerful that it ripped through the mine, causing instant death and destruction along its path. Eyewitnesses later reported seeing a ball of flame shoot some 60 metres into the sky. The smoke that followed created a mushroom cloud over the mine as if a nuclear bomb had hit it. The resulting blast wrecked the pithead. On the surface, workers were killed and buildings were levelled; most of them were left as nothing more than a pile of smouldering splinters. Witnesses said the site looked like a war zone.

Down in the mine, below the explosion site, Ken and the other miners in his immediate vicinity had no idea about what had just happened. "All we experienced down there was that big gust of wind. We know now that when the coal dust exploded, the fire raced to the surface in search of oxygen, and it went all the way to the top, where it broke through. But we didn't know that back then, so we kept working," Ken explains.

A few minutes after the rush of wind, Ken says he heard someone yelling, "Knock off! Knock off!" That was the recognized signal to immediately stop working because something had happened in the mine. "We knew then, that something wasn't right," Ken adds.

Following that signal, Ken and the other miners from that area headed out towards the surface. Still oblivious to the disaster above them, Ken says the men believed they could walk all the way to the top of the mine if they had to—but they quickly found out that wasn't going to happen.

"We had no sooner started out when we began smelling smoke and gas. The fumes were strong. The gas was hanging very heavy," he says. "When I went around a turn in the shaft, I heard someone holler, 'Don't go there. There's men dead out there.'"

Meeting with three or four other miners who had miraculously survived the blast, Ken said they decided that they would try to make their way up to the next level, because the gases were getting quite heavy where they were located. "We didn't know how much good air we had left, and we decided we had to do something, or else we feared we would die," he explains. The miners were able to break open an abandoned tunnel, and finally, after about an hour of digging and crawling through the rocks and coal, the men were able to get to the next level above.

"That's where we congregated in a small section of the mine," Ken explains.

On the surface, families who were eating dinner heard the wail of sirens—the traditional disaster signal in mining communities—and everyone from the tiny village instinctively knew there was tragedy afoot that evening. They raced to the mine to assist in the rescue effort. Upon their arrival, they could tell that the situation was bad, and they accepted that—although they held out hope for survivors—they knew this explosion would have tragic repercussions. It became painfully obvious that men were dead. Most likely many men.

Back underground, about 50 miners in total had made their way to the area where Ken and the four other miners had congregated. One of the new arrivals, a senior miner named Conrad Embree, had survived two other earlier mine disasters, and he used his experience and knowledge to guide the others. He instructed the miners to find anything they could get their hands on to build barricades to block off the mine shafts on either end and keep the gas from seeping in.

"We had congregated in this area behind what we called the 'trap door,' which they used to open to let coal dust out and good air to get into the mine," Ken recalls. "We got to the upside of that door and put a barricade up behind us trying to keep the gas away."

In this area, they found on the slope a 15-centimetre steel line that had been used in the mining operations to bring in compressed air to run the machines. Luckily, it was still functioning and pumping air into the mine. Using a hose, which the men stretched out and cut holes into, they could get air to breathe:

"By opening the valves, we could get air, and that gave us oxygen. That's what kept us going. On the other side of the door, there were men out there who were dead. We knew that, but there was nothing we could do for them. We knew they had been gassed. After an explosion and fire like there was down in that mine, the shafts were filled with carbon dioxide, and it's a deadly threat. They call it black damp gas. Three or four breaths of that and you're dead. The mine filled with it quickly, and, if you weren't killed in the fire, then you died from that gas. We were lucky to be alive, and we knew that."

Ken has no hesitation admitting he was frightened. "There I was, 19 years old and lying on the floor of a mine not knowing if I was going to live or die. Of course I was scared. Why wouldn't I be? It was scary as hell. We were all scared, we just didn't show it," he explains.

As time wore on, the men trapped underground tried their best to keep each other's spirits high. Sometimes they sang. Sometimes they talked about their families and fishing and things they liked to do. Some told jokes in an effort to distract each other. But mostly, as only miners in this situation can do, they waited. They waited for rescuers whom they knew would never give up on them. "We had no idea just how bad things were above us. All that night, we waited and hoped for someone to come and find us, but nothing happened. No one ever really gave up, but it was difficult," Ken concedes.

By Friday morning, the company confirmed that 13 miners were dead, and, although a search was being mounted to locate possible survivors, officials admitted they held out little hope of finding anyone alive in the stricken mine.

By Saturday, the rescuers, including both "barefaced" miners (without breathing apparatus) and "draegermen" (rescue workers), had reached the 975-metre level only to find a smouldering fire. There were no survivors there at that point. Fearing that a second explosion might occur with the buildup of gas, mine officials called the draeger teams out of the shafts, and the search was temporarily called off. Having already lost two rescuers when black damp gas got under their masks and killed them, they did not want to risk any more lives.

Later that Saturday, the company held a press conference. The general manager of coal operations met the media at the pithead and announced that in all probability there was no one still alive down in the mine. There was black damp gas, there was methane and a fire down in the mine, he explained.

Meanwhile, Ken says, on the second day, after the gas began to let up, one of the men decided to see how far up the shaft they could get. He didn't get far before he ran into cement water and came back to report his findings to the others. "We knew that meant the shaft was being sealed off. We knew that meant there was a fire above us, and that could be how they decided to fight that. Only a month earlier, there had been a mining accident in Germany, and they sealed the mine that way, but no one got out. Realizing this, all the men grew silent," Ken recalls. "We hoped that meant they were not giving up on us, but we knew if there was a bad fire, they had to do something to put it out. We were trapped, and we were at their mercy."

Ken notes that he believes that the officials honestly thought all of them were most likely dead. "They felt that it was near the stage that a second explosion was going to blow, and, if it did, they feared it would kill the rescuers. They felt they would seal the mine off and wait 24 hours to see what would happen. Their intentions may have been to seal it off permanently, but the rescuers were not going to have any of that. So the company agreed that they would seal the mine with the cement water, and, when they opened it the next day, if they found there was still gas in the mines, they would then seal it off permanently. That would have meant we would have been down there forever," Ken points out. "At this stage, it seems they really felt there wasn't any one alive down there."

Obviously, the company officials didn't know the resolve that these men had to live.

"I was cold, hungry and scared," Ken admits. "But I wasn't about to give up, and, like everyone else down there, I hoped the people on the surface wouldn't give up until we were safely out."

As luck would have it, an employee on the surface had been watching the valves and gauges on the compressor that had been used to pump air to the machines, and he noticed them fluctuating. "This guy manning the compression station went to the officials and told them that if they were going to close the mines for good, he wasn't going to have any part of it. He told them he felt there were still people alive down there, because he could see the hands on the compressor moving, which meant the air was being used. He told them he wasn't going to turn off the compressor. If anyone was going to do it, he said he felt it should be the general manager. Let him be the one to make the move, he said. Thank God this guy was on his toes and noticed those valves," Ken says gratefully.

Faced with the prospect that maybe there were some people alive down in the mine after all, the company changed its approach. After unsealing the mine once again, they decided to send the rescuers down through the No. 2 shaft and then in through the explosion doors. "Despite the presence of deadly gas and the risk to their own lives" Ken explains, "the rescuers pushed on, they dug deeper and deeper into the mine. Many of them were knocked unconscious by the gas, but still they pushed on, led by the draegermen, who cleared the way so the barefaced miners could come in. For every 15 men that went into the mine to help, they brought eight back out to the surface and sent them to the hospital—and once they were recovered only a few hours later, they'd be right back down there helping again."

Dr. Arnold Burden, a physician, was one of those rescuers who went barefaced into the mine, risking his life to save the men trapped so far below the surface. But talking about those experiences today, he says he never gave it a second thought. As a native of Springhill, he felt it was something he had to do. Dr. Burden had first worked in the mines as a teenager, and he continued to work there during the summer while he attended college and medical school.

In November 1956, when word of the Springhill Mine Explosion hit the news, Dr. Burden was practising medicine in Prince Edward Island. "When I heard about it, one of the first names of the men that they said was killed in the explosion was that of one of my best friends," Ken explains, "That's when I knew I had to come home to see what I could do to help."

After packing up his car with medical supplies, Dr. Burden caught the first ferry to Nova Scotia, arriving in Springhill late in the morning on November 2, the day after the explosion.

"It was as bad as I had expected it to be. We knew the explosion in the mine had been a bad one and that it had taken out the entire bankhead [entrance building]. We knew it was serious. With an explosion that bad, we knew there were going to be a lot of dead and injured, especially on the surface and in the bankhead. We also knew there were a lot of men unaccounted for," he recalls. "I was at the hospital looking after patients there when they called for a doctor to come to the mine to treat people there. I said I'd go."

When Dr. Burden arrived at the mine, he said he quickly determined there really wasn't anything he could do on the surface, so they suggested maybe he could do something down below. Despite the dangers that he knew he would encounter down there, he did not hesitate.

"I said, 'Sure, I'll do it.' I went and got a lamp and a pit suit and down I went." With his mining experience and knowing many of the men trapped or killed down in the shafts, he never paused for a minute. "I knew what could be down there, and I knew it could be dangerous, but it was just something I had to do," he attests.

The risks were great. Dr. Burden said he knew the gases could kill a man in seconds, and there was always the chance of another explosion. "I knew it would be a miracle if anyone had survived this, so I just felt I owed it to them to help get them out if there was anyone down there.

Rescuers were working in cramped quarters, and the doctor remembers it was tight going. "In most places, we only had a foot [30 centimetres] of crawl space with decent air. If you lifted your head any higher than a foot, you were in trouble. I actually passed out once for a few minutes when I lifted my head a few inches too high to offer assistance to one of the injured miners. It didn't take much for the gas to get you so you had to pay attention. We had to crawl on our bellies to get to these guys, and it was tough going."

❧◆☙

For the men in the mine, things looked grim, but, by late Sunday evening, after digging through metres of coal and several rockfalls, the rescuers finally reached the 1640-metre level.

For the men trapped in the mine, hearing the rescuers was music to their ears. Ken says it was a sound that he hears even to this day. "As long as I live, I will never forget hearing that thump on the trap door or what we saw when we opened it. It was a group of draegermen who told us help was on the way."

News of the survivors immediately flashed through town like a tornado. Now, Ken says, there was no such thing as closing the mine off.

"They worked and they worked and they worked trying to clear the gases until finally, that night, they got to us," Ken recalls, his cracking voice betraying his emotions. "When they began sending down soup and sandwiches, we knew we were finally going to get out. They worked through the night to get us out of there. When I heard those rescuers at the trap door, it was just like someone had told me I had won the lotto. There aren't words to describe how I felt. It really was a miracle that we survived, and it was a bigger miracle that they found us."

Rescuers started removing survivors from the mine through the No. 2 mine shortly after midnight on Monday, November 5. The CBC read the name of each man on the radio as he was brought to the surface. Ken Melanson was brought out at around 3:00 in the morning, and, sometime later that Monday morning, it was confirmed that they had found the last survivor. "If your name wasn't called, it meant you were dead," Ken says matter-of-factly.

Floyd Beaton and Richard Ellis, Ken's best friends, were among those who died and were still down there.

"That was pretty hard to take. I felt really bad for them. When the last man came out, they shut the mine down completely. They left all the bodies down in the mine because it was just too risky to send anyone down there to retrieve them. They just couldn't risk any more lives," Ken says.

The No. 2 and No. 4 shafts, which were connected, were both sealed until January 1957 to deprive the tunnels of oxygen and to allow the fires deeper in the mine to burn out. That January, the company began operations once again at the mine. They took steel coffins down into the shaft and brought out the bodies; the dead were taken to their homes because there were no funeral services such as we have today. "I remember seeing the crêpes [mourning cloths] on the doors of those homes; how sad it was," Ken recounts. "That meant there was a body in the house, and people would go visit and pay their respects to the families. It was a bad time."

As for Ken Melanson, he never went back down into the Springhill mines, but he worked for another five years at the nearby River Hebert coal mines. Years later, he went to work at the Springhill Coal Miners Museum and did his part to help keep alive the memories of those men who had died deep within the earth that day back in 1956.

At the time of the disaster, the entrance to the No. 4 mine was about 25 years old, and the tunnels went more than 1800 metres below the surface of the earth. Through the heroic work of the draegermen and bare-faced miners alike who had raced to rescue the miners trapped underground, 88 miners in total had been brought out, with 52 coming from deep inside the mine on the third day after the disaster. In the final tally, the explosion in the No. 4 mine was found to have claimed the lives of 39 men.

As tragic as the events of 1956 were, less than two years later the scene of devastation was to be repeated. During its course, the little town of Springhill managed to capture the attention of the whole continent—that story is next.

Springhill Mine Disaster
(The Bump)

October 23, 1958
Springhill, Nova Scotia

D R. ARNOLD BURDEN, A FAMILY physician who had grown up in Springhill and worked in the famous coal mines as a teenager to help pay his way through college, was seeing to patients in his Springhill office when he heard the first thump. It was a very distinct noise, he recalls. At first, he thought it was thunder. Then the first thump was immediately followed by a second, and then, right after it, there was a third thump. Thinking back on it now, the doctor says the noises sounded somewhat as if three bombs had been dropped on the town, but, instinctively, he knew what it was.

"My first thought was, 'No, not again,'" he recalls. "'It can't be the mine again, not after what we had just gone through not even two years ago.'"

But, to the shock and dismay of Dr. Burden and all the townsfolk of Springhill, they soon learned that, indeed, yet another tragedy had occurred at the mine.

On October 23, 1958, the Springhill "Bump" left a legacy of death and destruction that devastated the entire town.

So, what exactly is a bump? A bump typically happens in an area that has been heavily mined. Over time, tunnel support pillars can weaken, shift and collapse, often as a result of earth tremors or new excavations. With the supports gone, stresses in the rock can cause the walls or floors of shafts to shift, crushing anyone unlucky enough to be in the area and sealing the shaft.

By October 1958, the Springhill No. 2 Colliery was one of the deepest mines in the world. It extended more than 4260 metres below the earth's surface into some of the richest coal deposits in North America. The first major bump occurred at 8:06 PM on October 23, and two shockwaves, which would have felt like earthquakes, rippled through the mine. The shift was felt at the surface, and draegermen (rescue workers) and barefaced (without breathing apparatus) miners were quickly dispatched into the shafts to survey the damage and rescue any survivors. Below 3960 metres, they found men slowly making their way towards the surface. Below 4200 metres, they discovered that the ceiling had collapsed. Many miners had been crushed by the falling rock. Making matters worse, dangerous levels of gas were now being released.

From his office, Dr. Burden went directly to the pithead to see what was going on. "I knew there wasn't much I could do until they figured out what had happened down there. By 9:00, two draeger teams, myself and a mine official were on our way down into the mine. We encountered some minor gas pockets along the way, but nothing serious like the explosion of two years earlier, when we had to crawl on our bellies to avoid being overtaken by the poisonous gases. We kept going down the slope, and we were down quite a ways when we encountered the first dead man," the doctor recalls. He was the only dead miner that the team would come across.

"The further down we went, the more damage we found as we began to see where the mine's floor rose up to meet the ceiling," he says. "Think of it this way. You're in a room, and suddenly the floor rises up to meet the ceiling. If you were in there, you would have been killed instantly. That's what happened to any of the miners who would have been in those shafts when that earth moved. They would have been killed instantly, there isn't much doubt about that," Dr. Burden explains. "I really believe those men would not have known what hit them."

Caleb Rushton, a 35-year-old husband and father of two small children, thought that October 23, 1958, was going to be a routine day. As things turned out, nothing whatsoever about this particular day would be routine.

Scheduled to work the afternoon shift, which started at 4:00 PM, Caleb got up that day around 9:00 AM. He spent the morning doing routine chores around the house, and after a nice lunch prepared by his wife, he got ready to head for the mines. About an hour before his shift was to begin, Caleb's wife drove him to the mine, where he went to the miner's cabin and changed into his pit clothes. Then he caught the trolley that took him far below the surface. Arriving at his work site at around 4:00, Caleb went about his duties, oblivious to any impending danger. It was a routine he had carried out for many years, having worked in the coal mines since he was a teenager. At this point, he estimates that he was about 3960 metres underground and working on a 35-degree slope; the mineshafts were typically at angles, not level.

"At about five minutes past eight, I was leaning up against a wall, waiting for timber to come down the shaft that I would then pass onto to the next fellow so that they could use it on the wall down in the next level," Caleb recalls.

"I really don't know what happened next," he continues. "I never seen anything, never felt anything, never heard anything or realized anything was wrong until I was coming to [gaining consciousness]. When I came around, I was leaning against my pack up against a wall with my legs stretched out straight in front of me. By instinct, I guess, I was hollering pretty loud because some rocks had fallen on my legs and I was having a hard time moving them," Caleb observes.

Thankfully, he notes, the rocks did not seriously injure his legs.

"Suddenly, I heard somebody hollering back at me, telling me to calm down and to take it easy," Caleb recalls. "They told me to try to relax and that they would get to me as fast as they could, but first they had to move some rocks before they could get to where I was."

In time, several miners made their way to Caleb's location and dug him free, carefully removing the rocks from his legs so as not to cause him any injury. "Then, once I was freed, we all started looking for other miners who might need our help. We knew there had been a bump, and we could tell things were bad," Caleb explains.

After a few minutes of groping around in the dusty darkness, Caleb says they were able to locate several men. Eventually, 12 miners were gathered together in a confined space thousands of metres below the surface with no apparent way out. Luckily, he adds, there were no critical injuries within their group.

"One fellow had a broken shoulder, and another fellow had a broken leg, but, other than that, we were pretty lucky that no one was in serious pain," he comments. "The rest of us were not in too bad shape, but we didn't know exactly what had happened in the mine at that time. We knew we were in trouble, but we had no idea just how serious it was."

Caleb and the others made the two injured men as comfortable as possible, considering the circumstances. "We knew there had been a really bad bump that had pushed the floor right up to the ceiling all around us except for this small area we were in," he explains. "Imagine taking a pipe and squeezing it together until there's no space in the centre. That's what this was like. We figured this is what probably happened to the shafts, especially to the ones just above us and just below us."

Hoping to gain a better understanding of their predicament, the trapped miners fanned out along the mine wall, feeling their way in the darkness so as to conserve their lamps. They first moved as far as they could up the shaft until they reached the blockage. It was about 60 metres from their original location. They could go no farther. They then moved down the shaft, repeating the procedure, but they didn't get far before they ran into another blockage.

"But luckily, down there we discovered the compressor air pipe. It had been snapped off at that spot, but it was still moving air. We made a plan that we would all take turns going back to that pipe and holler into it on regular intervals in the hopes that our voices would carry to the surface and someone up there would hear us and they would know we were alive down there," he says. "In the end, it turned out that only two or three of us did that, but it made us feel that we were actually doing something. It wasn't much, but at least we were trying... Besides, what else did we have to do?"

As time crawled by, Caleb says the miners knew they were in serious trouble, but no one panicked. "Everyone seemed to accept the situation we were in, but they never gave up hoping that we would get rescued. I really believe

Two of the men to emerge from the Springhill mines following the October 23, 1958 accident known as the Bump. A total of 74 miners were killed in this mining disaster.

that every man down there felt in his heart that we would get out. I kept thinking that even though I didn't know how long it would be before we were rescued, I just felt we were going to be okay. I maintained that belief right from the start. I never gave up hope, and I guess maybe that's what got me through all those days even as we began to realize that the more time that went by, the chances of us being rescued grew more faint. But hope was all we had."

To pass the time, they talked, sang and told jokes and stories, but mostly the miners kept their thoughts to themselves. "I guess in a time like that, there really isn't much you can say, is there?" Caleb conceded.

After five days of being trapped under kilometres of rock and coal, the miners finally had their prayers answered. "On the fifth day, one of the other miners, Gordie, was hollering out the pipe when someone from above hollered back. Our plan had worked. Someone had actually heard us on the outside...It was a miracle."

As it turned out, on the surface, one of the mine surveyors had heard Gordie's screams and came to the pipe. "He asked us how many men were down there, and we told him. Then he told us to sit tight and to hang on, that help was on the way. He said it would be a while before they could get to us because they had to dig through virgin coal to reach us. I think it was about 68 feet [21 metres] of the stuff, and that was tough going. We knew they would get to us as soon as they could, but they couldn't go too fast because they didn't want to cause a cave-in," Caleb explains.

Caleb admits it is difficult to put into words how he felt when he heard that man's voice from the surface.

> "At that point, we were okay with waiting until they could get to us. The important thing now was that they knew we were alive down there. Through all of this, and even today, I keep thanking God that that pipe was there because if it had not been for that pipe, who can say how things might have turned out. The pipe wasn't used for breathing air. We had lots of air from the big fans on the back slope. Luckily for us, they were still working, but it was a good thing they found us when they did because our food and water supply was long gone. In a situation like that, you don't mind the hunger so much; it's the thirst that really gets to you. Especially in a coal mine, with all that dust in your mouth. It certainly wasn't pleasant, I can tell you that much."

Having located the stranded miners, to tide them over until they could be rescued, the rescuers pushed a tube down the pipe, and through it they then ran water and soup to the trapped men. "So at least that meant we could get a drink of water and have something to eat," Caleb says. "I tell you, it was a godsend."

The next morning at around 5:00, some six and a half days after the men became trapped below the surface, rescuers finally broke through the coal wall and started removing the survivors on stretchers. "I think that was the best feeling I ever had in my life. There really is no way to describe how that felt," Caleb recounts.

Describing the mixed emotions he has when he thinks back on that moment, Caleb explains, "Of course I was thankful to be alive, and I knew just how lucky I was. When I think about all those other men who were lost down there, it does make me feel awkward, but I also know there was nothing we could do about it. It was just one of those things that was meant to be. I count my blessings every day."

For Caleb, getting rescued from the pit was the end of the line for his coal-mining career. He had twice escaped death from the mines, and he knew, if there should be a third time, he might not be so lucky. He wasn't about to take the chance and gamble with his life. He had a family counting on him, and he wouldn't risk putting them through that another time.

He had been working in the lamp cabin when the mine had exploded two years earlier, and he knew he had been lucky to survive the blast. Many of the men on the surface had not been so fortunate.

"But, in the summer of 1957, I had to go back down the mine after it was reopened following the explosion because my job in the lamp cabin had been taken away," he says. "I really didn't want to go, but I had no choice.

I had a family, and I needed the job. Faced with that situation, you have to do what you have to do," he states.

Caleb realizes that he was lucky to have escaped the second disaster with only minor scratches to his legs from the rocks that had fallen on him and with a bump on his head from where he had hit the wall; other than that, he was physically okay. However, he explains, "I had nightmares for a while after the disaster, but after a few years they went away. But I never complained about any of that. I knew I had nothing to complain about."

Some miners had been rescued much sooner than Caleb and his companions. By 4:00 in the morning of the day following the bump, on October 24, 75 survivors had been brought out of the mine. The rescue teams continued the search for survivors, but the collapse made for a lot of debris to move through. Those on the surface prayed for a repeat of the miracle from the 1956 explosion; they held out hope that others would be rescued.

Meanwhile, the media descended upon the town in one of the first tragedies ever to be televised. Rescue teams had come from other coal-mining communities in Cape Breton and Pictou County to help with the massive effort.

Finally, on October 29, more than five days after the bump occurred, rescuers made contact with Caleb's group of trapped miners. After tunnelling through 49 metres of rock, in the early morning hours of October 30, rescue workers reached the group of 12 men. Another group of survivors was found the next day, but they would be the last of the men to come safely out of the Springhill No. 2 mine. There were 174 men in the mine at the time of the bump, and a total of 100 came out alive.

Following the second disaster in as many years, the Dominion Steel and Coal Corporation ended its operations in Springhill, putting the majority of the town's men out of work. It took years for the employment situation to stabilize, and Springhill's population decreased from more than 7300 in 1956 to roughly 6000 in 1964.

Crash of Arrow Air
Flight 1285

December 12, 1985
Gander, Newfoundland

DECEMBER 12, 1985, PROMISED to be a cold and damp day for Newfoundland. As dawn was breaking, a heavy fog hung in the air, embracing everything it touched with a moist hug. Freezing rain had just finished pelting the countryside, blanketing most surfaces with a sleek layer of ice. Just before sunrise, an Arrow Air DC-8 rolled onto the runway at Gander International Airport. A few minutes later, now a fiery projectile of death, it crashed into the hillside near Gander Lake. In an instant, all 256 souls on board—248 American soldiers and 8 civilian flight crew—were killed.

The small town of Gander is situated in the northeastern part of the island of Newfoundland. It owes its existence to the aviation facility now known as Gander International Airport. The result of international discussions begun in 1933, the airport was designed as a refuelling station for the first commercial transatlantic flights, which were expected to be technologically possible in several years. Construction began in 1936 and took nearly three years to complete. To support the workers, a town developed in what had previously been wilderness.

By the time the airport, which was among the world's largest, was complete and awaiting its first transatlantic planes, World War II was underway. Recognizing the strategic value of the facility, the Royal Canadian Air Force took over, made improvements and used it as a base for antisubmarine forays and as a jumping-off point for Europe-bound flights. Up to 15,000 people at a time could be found in Gander during this period.

After the war, the airport reverted to civilian use, and a new townsite, incorporated in 1958, was constructed at a safer distance from it. Meanwhile, commercial transatlantic flights became a reality. For many years, Gander was known as the "Crossroads of the World" because almost all flights between North America and Europe would stop there to refuel. Then, as new planes with larger fuel tanks came into use, fewer flights stopped in Gander, and it began a slow slide back into relative obscurity.

Gander would once again be thrust to the forefront of world attention on September 11, 2001, though. When the first hijacked jets began crashing into prominent United States buildings, the aviation authorities took the unprecedented precautionary step of ordering all planes in North American airspace to land immediately. Gander's combination of long runways, ample aircraft parking and isolated location proved ideal; 39 of 239 diverted transatlantic flights to land in Canada came there. For up to three days, while the crisis was resolved, about 6600 passengers and aircraft crew members found themselves stranded at Gander. Rising to the occasion, with characteristic Newfoundland hospitality, the people of Gander and nearby communities opened their hearts and jumped in with Operation Yellow Ribbon to provide food, shelter and even entertainment to their unexpected guests for the duration.

However, it is the fate of Arrow Air Flight 1285, some 16 years earlier, that concerns us here.

Shortly after 6:45 on the morning of December 12, 1985, Greg Seward, a reporter and photographer at the Gander *Beacon,* the town's weekly newspaper, received a call from a friend advising him that he may want to quickly get over to the airport because something big was going on. Only minutes earlier, the caller informed Greg, there had been a major plane crash near Gander Lake, just outside the airport perimeter.

Greg recalls he was stunned at the news. With Gander being an airport town, emergency personnel, local authorities and certain other community members constantly trained for such disasters—as well as many other tragic scenarios—but no one ever imagined that such a tragedy would really occur.

"In fact, ironically, we had actually rehearsed such a scenario less than a month earlier—what do we do if a commercial airliner crashes outside the airport fence? All the major response agencies and the media were involved in the training exercise," Greg explains. "Of course the media has a role to play in any situation like this. If such a thing were to happen, any response would have to involve the entire community, so we were all prepared."

Or at least they thought they were prepared, Greg quickly admits, but it isn't possible to be fully prepared for something of this magnitude.

The article below, which appeared in the December 18, 1985, edition of the *Beacon,* told the story:

> *"The worst plane crash on Canadian soil in history occurred in Gander just before 7:00 last Thursday morning, taking 256 American lives. There were no survivors.*

"*The crash came shortly after the Miami, Florida, Arrow Airlines DC-8 jetliner, under charter to the United States Defence Department, took off from Gander, where it had taken on some 100,000 pounds [45,360 kilograms] of fuel. It had left Runway 22, which ends near the Trans-Canada Highway, but the plane, carrying 248 members, three of them women, of the 101st Airborne Division to their home base at Fort Campbell, Kentucky, barely made it a quarter of a mile [400 metres], coming down near Gander Lake. There were also eight crewmembers.*

"*The actual location was off a dirt road, known as the boating house road, which is maintained by Transport Canada, that operates the Gander International Airport. The road leads to boathouse facilities of the department, located at the side of the lake. The plane struck a small hill, then bellied for some 300 yards [275 metres], while it split in pieces and the main section came to rest amid intense smoke and fire. Bodies, clothes, luggage and cargo, generally, were strewn over the path, left through the wooden area.*

"*The U.S. military personnel, who were returning to spend Christmas with their families at Hopkinsville, Kentucky, had been on assignment as a peacekeeping force in the Sinai Peninsula of Egypt. The plane had left Cairo, Egypt, then stopped over at Cologne, West Germany, before continuing on to Gander. At the time of the crash, [the] weather was overcast, and there was freezing rain overnight.*

"*An all-out search began into cause of the crash, as a 300-member search team arrived from Washington and Ottawa. The black box flight recorders were found but were damaged, so there was no immediate indication of what caused the crash.*

"For Gander, it was quite a week as the tragic and traumatic drama unfolded. News reporting teams from all parts of North America descended on Gander, the likes of which were never seen before. Some of the teams arrived in private jets. As soon as the crash was reported, local news representatives rushed to the Gander airport, where they were briefed by airport general manager John Pittman. Among them were representatives from the Beacon.

"After the briefing, at 8:30 AM, the local news representatives, through the cooperation of Mr. Pittman, were taken to the crash scene by Transport Canada guide official Pat Kane. Following this visit, the scene was closed to all members of the news media, from a ground surface view, for two days. Search officials feared for explosions, fearing there was ammunition aboard the aircraft. There was nothing removed from the crash site until Friday. A hangar served as a make-shift morgue.

"From the Gander community side of the situation, the hospital was alerted, but, as grim details came to light, it was soon indicated that there were no survivors, which meant there was no emergency need for the hospital. The crash caused a small fuel leak in Gander Lake, source of the town's water supply, but this was taken care of.

"Investigation into the crash was the responsibility of the Canadian Aviation Safety Board, and there would be a public inquiry.

"In Beirut, an anonymous caller, who claimed to be representing the Islamic Jihad organization, said this group caused the crash. There was another such claim, as well, but all were dismissed by both the RCMP and United States government officials.

"The soldiers who died in the crash were members of the Third Battalion, 202nd Infantry, at Fort Campbell. Hopkinsville has a population of 28,000, and Mayor Sherril Jeffers said he was heartbroken in sympathy for the bereaved families. There is a close relationship between the town and base, he noted.

"During the refuelling stopover at Gander, personnel went to the Gander terminal, some of them making purchases at the duty-free shop. In some instances, souvenir T-shirts were purchased, reading, in a light touch: I survived Gander, Newfoundland.

"It was the worst air crash in Gander since 1967, when a Czechoslovakian plane went down, killing 38 people."

More than 20 years later, Greg still has vivid memories of what he saw, heard and experienced early that morning.

Greg notes that, after getting the tip about the crash from his friend, "I actually even received an official call from the emergency response team who had been assembled for such a scenario. But by this time...[I] was just getting ready to go out the door on my way to the airport."

After the calls, Greg went immediately and directly to the airport, where he was to rendezvous at a prearranged location with other media representatives. "This was all part of the plan. We knew we were supposed to assemble at this specific hangar in the event of such an emergency. That's where I went."

Greg clearly remembers the weather that December day. "Very cold. There had been freezing rain earlier in the morning—maybe around 3:00 or 4:00. That's where a lot of this confusion and speculation comes from. A lot of people said that ice must have brought the plane down, because they had to scrape their car that morning. But I don't buy that. In fact, the freezing rain had stopped even before the aircraft landed in Gander, and it didn't start up again until after it crashed. There's no way there was any ice build-up on that plane, but I will agree it was a pretty miserable morning as far as weather goes."

At the media meeting in its prearranged place, the authorities gave a brief explanation of what had happened, and airport personnel agreed to take several reporters to the scene. Seven reporters, representing a variety of media outlets—including Greg on behalf of the *Beacon*—piled into the airport manager's car and headed to the crash location for what turned out to be a five-minute visit.

Thinking back on the short time he had at the crash site, Greg describes it as something out of a nightmare:

"It was a scene of utter and total devastation. The plane had crashed in a heavily wooded area, but it had pretty much been cleared when the plane went down. A fireball came down the hill and just levelled everything in its path. It sheared off trees, it knocked them down and flattened them out. It was like a blast effect, with the trees angled back from the centre of impact. Obviously, I had never seen anything remotely like that before in my life. I thought it looked very odd. There was an eerie atmosphere around everything. It was cold that morning, but the ground felt warm, and the air around the crash site felt warm. A heavy haze from the lake and thick smoke from the fire were both hanging over the area. There didn't seem to be a breath of wind.

It was deathly quiet except that you could hear the echo
of the firefighters yelling up and down the crash site.
But, overall, the silence was heavy."

Beyond the quiet, Greg says the images were difficult
to observe, but they are forever seared into his memory.
"From where we stood that morning, we could see bodies and parts of bodies...The absolute devastation is hard
to describe. There were places where there was a green,
bushy tree with a body that was lying on top of it that
was burned to a crisp. Then, 6 feet [2 metres] away from
that, there would be a tree burned to a crisp with a body
laying on it that wasn't even singed. It just didn't make
sense. It was like the whole world got put into a bag,
shook up and dumped out. It was a total mess. I don't
know how else to describe it," he continues. "When you
see something like that, you have no way of putting it
into context, so it becomes difficult to register. It's hard to
put a scene like that into perspective. You just can't find
the right words. It's hard to describe the feelings and
emotions you're dealing with. I think I just tried to let it
slip out of my mind, but of course there are some things
that you can just never forget."

The official story has it that Arrow Air Flight 1285,
a McDonnell Douglas DC-8, crashed after takeoff from
Newfoundland's Gander International Airport at 6:45 AM
on December 12, 1985. Because of the large amount of fuel
on board—the plane was flying direct from Gander to Fort
Campbell, Kentucky—it took nearly four hours for the firefighters who responded to bring the blaze under control. It
was more than a day before the flames were completely
extinguished, according to a historical summary released
by the United States Department of the Army in 1986.

All passengers on board were American servicemen returning from the Mount Sinai region. Most were members of the 101st Airborne Division (Air Assault) who had just completed a six-month tour of duty in the Middle East with the Multinational Force and Observers, a peace-keeping force made up of parties from 10 different countries. The force had been responsible for enforcing the security provisions contained in the 1979 Israel–Egypt peace accord.

The Canadian Aviation Safety Board immediately began an investigation into the crash. Initially, it was believed that a combination of factors, not the least of which was ice on the wings, might have contributed to the crash. However, a further investigation by a nine-member panel failed to come to a truly definitive conclusion as to the cause of the crash. The majority, five members, stated that sufficient evidence existed to indicate that, shortly after takeoff, the aircraft stalled because of excessive drag, possibly the result of ice, creating a situation in which the plane was, for all intents and purposes, doomed—especially given the amount of fuel on board.

However, four other members, including two aeronautical engineers, believed that the evidence suggested a completely different cause. In part, the dissenters stated in their minority report, "...we cannot agree—indeed, we categorically disagree—with the majority findings... The evidence shows that the Arrow Air DC-8 suffered an on-board fire and a massive loss of power before it crashed... The fire may have been associated with an in-flight detonation from an explosive or incendiary device." Supporting the minority viewpoint were autopsy reports that revealed that some soldiers had inhaled smoke before perishing.

Zona Phillips, the Florida stepmother of 23-year-old Sergeant Doug Phillips—who was one of the Gander crash victims—established a group called Families for Truth About Gander. Her goal was to get to the bottom of the dissenting opinion on the cause of the Gander crash— even it if meant exposing a cover-up.

Greg agrees that the conflicting findings raise serious doubts about the "official" cause of the plane crash. He says his suspicions were aroused within minutes of arriving at the crash site that December morning.

"It was a disaster scene, so of course there would be police around," Greg begins, "but this felt different to me and not at all like I would have expected. Although they had told us we could have 15 minutes, we weren't there any longer than five minutes when this big, burley RCMP officer comes barrelling over toward us and yelling for us to get out of there. He told the airport people that we didn't need to be there, that we had no business being there. At the time, there was great concern that there might have been weapons on board the plane, since the passengers were soldiers. We didn't know it at the time, but there was not supposed to be any ammunition or weapons of any kind on board that aircraft, but here we were ducking bullets. There's no mistaking what it was. Of course, they would never admit it, but there were explosions and bullets going off all around us and small arms chattering in the woods all around the crash site. This was still less than two hours after the crash, and, when the firefighters first got there, they told us it was like a war zone with bullets going off," he explains.

Although Greg says he has heard all the "official" explanations for the crash, he insists that there are things about the tragedy that just do not add up.

"I don't mean to trample on anyone's beliefs, but there was substantial evidence and eyewitness reports that suggest there was a pre-impact explosion on board that plane. Several eyewitnesses reported seeing flames on the plane before it hit the ground—yet, officially, no one will confirm that," he says. "Coincidently, every scrap of evidence that would support this belief had disappeared within two days of the crash. There were parts of that plane that showed impact from the inside out, suggesting high-impact explosives were on board. All this evidence was either missed, ignored or shuffled away into a hangar or buried out at the landfill, and witnesses were discredited. The response was really quite frightening, when you think of it, considering the implications."

And Greg wonders why the authorities would have so quickly dismissed the possibility of a terrorist bomb on the plane.

"*The* [alleged terrorist group Islamic] *Jihad tried to claim responsibility three times for the crash, and they were ignored each time in favour of this theory of wing icing, which really is harmless in most cases. It's also interesting to note that this is the same time that* [United States military aide] *Oliver North was shipping illegal arms in the Iranian–Contra affair. There is reason to believe that North may have used this particular Arrow aircraft to transport those shipments. We didn't know it at the time, but the rule is that if the military is going to ship weapons, they have to use their own planes, but we know they didn't. This was a commercial passenger jetliner with a civilian crew that had been hired by the military. There was not supposed to be a single bullet on that plane, but yet we know there was about two and a half tonnes of ordnance recovered,*

never mind those which would have blown up in the
fire after the crash."

Although Greg says he understands the need for security around the crash site, he questions the size of that force that was used. "As we were being taken off that site, we met soldiers armed with submachine guns heading in to guard the site. I can't help wondering just what they were guarding. We know the site was sealed off for 48 hours after the crash. Only military personnel were allowed in. We know they lugged a lot of stuff onto a plane, and that aircraft flew off, taking evidence with it. After that, they came back and said there were no explosives on that plane. I say there was. I was the one out there dodging bullets that morning. I know what I saw and heard," Greg says firmly.

"My personal belief is that it was a terrorist bomb [that brought the plane down]," Greg asserts with conviction. "There is every reason to believe that those terrorists were telling the truth when they called to claim responsibility. They followed the same pattern as other terrorists in other attacks," he continues. "Why discount this report? Why would Canada go along with the U.S. on this [cover-up]? It's a Big-Brother thing. I believe that if Canadian authorities were told it was necessary for reasons of national security, I can see them going along with it."

Today, Greg works for the Town of Gander as communications development officer and media coordinator, and he says the events of the tragic plane crash will forever remain a part of the community's fabric. "It was a terrible time for the town," he says.

"People wanted to help, but they felt helpless. We are
an airport town, we know these things can happen. We
are always prepared for something to happen. We had
dealt with several incidents over the years, but certainly

not anything like that. The plan was in place. Everyone knew what to do. One of the most devastating effects on the community, I think, was that there was nothing they could do to help the people on the plane. There was an incredible instant response, but when rescue personnel got there, they quickly discovered there was absolutely nothing they could do to help, and I think that's the feeling that went throughout the entire community. It was very much a feeling of helplessness. Here we were, a community wanting to help, but there was no one [for us] to help. It was such a terrible feeling.

"Frustration was another emotion people were experiencing. The people were numb, praying for survivors. To sit back and watch without being able to help was totally devastating for the people of Gander. It was so overwhelming, so beyond our normal experiences, that after awhile I think most people just shut down and reacted on impulse. It was a terrible tragedy, and the memories live on with those who experienced it."

The Town of Gander marked the 20th anniversary of the air crash tragedy with a special ceremony on December 12, 2005. The event included a wreath-laying ceremony at the Silent Witness Memorial, which has been built at the crash site near Gander Lake.

As of this writing, with its 256 dead, the Arrow Air disaster resulted in the highest single-day death toll suffered by the United States Armed Forces since the end of World War II, and it remains the deadliest ever plane crash on Canadian soil. (Disconcertingly, the investigation surrounding the bombing of Air India Flight 182, which killed 329, including 160 Canadians, off the coast of Ireland on June 23 of the same year, is also still controversial.)

An editorial that appeared in the Gander *Beacon* a week
after the crash best sums up the Arrow Air Disaster:

> *"Having an international airport can sure bring
> a community close to world situations. No such com-
> munity knows this better than Gander, as witnessed by
> this latter* [most recent] *terrible plane crash. For
> Gander is not always tuned in, as it were, but is some-
> times even part of these world situations themselves, as
> well.*

> *"The peculiar part about this relationship with the
> world is that life can be so casual in a community the
> size of Gander one moment, then the whole world
> breaks loose, as they say. Nothing speaks more* [of] *this
> than the incident last Thursday.*

> *"The town was awakening from the usual night
> slumber to be instantly informed of a plane crash.
> Then, from that moment, the grim details unfolded. For
> witnesses, like the police, firemen, government officials,
> reporters and photographers, who were on the scene
> early, it was soon evident that the prospect of finding
> any passenger at all alive was remote. Scattered bodies
> spoke for the horror of it all.*

> *"But even a tragic situation is not without a stir of
> pride. We are proud of how our community can face up
> to these situations as it did in 1967* [when the Czech-
> oslovakian plane went down]*…In other respects,
> too, Gander as a whole and from the community per-
> spective is known to rise well to world situations, which
> serve to denote longtime relationships and also a matu-
> rity that has grown with time.*

> *"Meanwhile, we would like to extend deepest sympa-
> thy to the bereaved families of the plane crash, knowing
> too well the shock and grief they have to bear."*

Every time a tragedy—no matter how big—has struck in their midst, the people of Atlantic Canada have reached out to help others. Thrust into the aftermath of what is one of the largest disasters in Newfoundland history, the residents of Gander unselfishly answered the call.

Westray Mine Explosion

May 9, 1992
Plymouth, Nova Scotia

IT IS 5:18 ON THE MORNING of May 9, 1992. Deep within the bowels of the earth near Plymouth, Nova Scotia, 26 men go about their duties, digging coal in the dark, congested shafts of the Westray mine, oblivious to the events unfolding around them.

One of the men working a seam of coal in the southwestern section of the mine cuts through the rock in an effort to extract the valuable substance that nature has nurtured down here for thousands of years. As he drives his pick into the coalface, sparks fly. Sparks are not unusual. It happens all the time. Every miner in this place would have seen his share of sparks. However, this time, one of the errant sparks ignites a pocket of methane gas that has been building within the coal mine. As the flash fire ignites the coal dust that has been stirred up by the workers, the flames quickly spread out through the mine. Racing along the shafts as if on a mission, the flames embrace everything in their path. Seconds later, the mine explodes with powerfully destructive force. In an instant, all the miners inside are killed, and the shockwaves are felt several kilometres away.

One witness compared the blast to the firing of a rifle with all the force coming out of the end of the barrel.

At almost the same time, Allen Martin is returning home from doing the back shift (between the afternoon and morning shifts) at the local paper mill when he passes through the nearby town of Stellarton. As he approaches the local grocery store, he is curious to note several vehicles in the parking lot. He thinks it odd that so many people would be out and about at so early an hour. He soon sees that a crowd has assembled on the nearby riverbank, and that many of the people are using binoculars to look across to the other side as if searching for something. Slowing his vehicle in an effort to catch a glimpse of whatever these people are looking for, he cannot see anything out the ordinary. He thinks about stopping to ask someone what the fuss is all about, but he is tired after his shift, and all he wants to do is sleep. He shrugs off the unusual sight and drives away.

Heading directly home, Allen immediately goes to bed. Within minutes of turning off the lights, however, the telephone rings. Scrambling to answer the phone before the ringing wakes his wife, Debbie, he wonders who could possibly be calling at this hour.

"Hello," he stammers, trying to contain his displeasure at having to answer the phone instead of being in bed.

It's his brother. He informs Allen that there has been a terrible accident, an explosion at the mine. He asks Allen if he knows if their younger brother, Glenn, had been scheduled to work that night.

Shocked by the news, Allen somehow answers, telling his brother he has no idea if Glenn was working, but he promises to find out and get back to him.

Suddenly, the image of the cars in the parking lot of the Stellarton grocery store flood back into his mind, and in an instant it all makes sense.

Quickly getting dressed, Allen and Debbie decide they will not call his parents to get them alarmed, at least not until they have more information to share. After all, it is possible that Glenn was not working this night. Even if he were scheduled to be there, it wasn't unusual for the men to switch shifts.

Eventually, though, after going to the mine's parking area to locate Glenn's truck, Allen is faced with little choice. Going to the home of his elderly parents, he wakes them and gets them out of bed. Yes, they tell Allen, Glenn was working this night.

That's how Allen's nightmare began, and, even to this day, he recalls the events of that dreadful night just as vividly as if they were happening right now. His brother, Glenn, died that night, just two days before his 36th birthday.

But he did not perish alone. Killed in the blast along with Glenn David Martin were John Thomas Bates, Larry Arthur Bell, Bennie Joseph Benoit, Wayne Michael Conway, Ferris Todd Dewan, Adonis Joseph Dollimont, Robert Steven Doyle, Remi Joseph Drolet, Roy Edward Feltmate, Charles Robert Fraser, Myles Daniel Gillis, John Philip Halloran, Randolph Brian House, Trevor Martin Jahn, Laurence Elwyn James, Eugene William Johnson, Stephen Paul Lilley, Michael Frederick MacKay, Angus Joseph MacNeil, Harry Alliston McCallum, Eric Earl McIsaac, George James Munroe, Danny James Poplar, Romeo Andrew Short and Peter Francis Vickers.

The Westray coal mine of Plymouth, Nova Scotia, began operation on September 11, 1991. The last coal mine in Pictou County had ceased operation in the 1970s, and it was believed that Westray offered a new chance for prosperity. Today, all that remains of that promised prosperity are the shattered lives of the families of the miners who perished in the explosion and the hope that the lessons learned from this disaster will prevent a repeat of the tragedy.

Dean Jobb, an award-winning investigative journalist and author, was sent to Plymouth to cover the mine disaster for the province's daily newspaper, the Halifax *Chronicle-Herald*. Jobb has spent years researching and writing about the Westray disaster and its resulting fall-out. His book, *Calculated Risk: Greed, Politics and the Westray Tragedy,* is considered the definitive story of the Westray mining disaster. He describes it as the classic scenario for a mining accident. The experts have made it clear that there was some kind of flash fire down in the mineshafts that night, he says. Investigations after the explosion concluded that the fire was obviously sparked by methane gas and that the situation was compounded by coal dust that had built up in the air.

That's how the explosion happened, but Jobb says it shouldn't have.

"You have laws and equipment to deal with the flushing and ventilation of methane and coal dust, because it's a deadly combination. If the methane reaches between five and 15 percent in concentration in the air, it can combust. And if there's coal dust present to act as fuel, well, then, you have a disaster such as the one at Westray," he explains. "It just shouldn't happen."

Initially, it might have been possible to contain the methane fire, but the resulting flames from that fire would have stirred into the air and ignited the coal dust. Together, Jobb says, they would have created a second-ary, even more powerful explosion. "Just the descriptions from witnesses and nearby residents who told of the earth shaking and of people being startled from their sleep gives us an idea of the force of the explosion...We know that it was tremendous. Basically, in a confined space like that, there was only one way out for the force, and that was through the surface," Jobb explains.

When the blast broke the surface, some officials said it would have been much like an erupting volcano, with the earth expelling fire, smoke, soot, rocks and debris from everything the rolling force had picked up along the way.

"And of course we now know there were 26 men down there in that mine," Jobb says. "Coroners later concluded that the men would have died within seconds of the blast, either killed by the flames or overcome by the fumes and gases. It was a tragedy, a needless loss of life."

In the days and weeks that followed the explosion, there was a tremendous amount of shock and grief in the community and throughout all of Nova Scotia.

For Allen Martin and the other families of the men trapped in the mine, the few days immediately following the explosion were among the worst days of their lives. As Jobb notes, "The days that followed were painful. It's so hard to put into words, but it was like we were all living in some terrible dream. We just walked around in a daze all the time, waiting for word about our loved ones," Jobb recalls. "We all had hope that somehow, by some miracle, they would have survived the blast. That's all we had at that point."

It was an agonizing waiting game for the families, Jobb says. A terrible, excruciatingly painful waiting game with answers becoming hard to find. They hoped. They prayed for a miracle, but there would be no miracle amid this tragedy.

Two days after the blast, rescuers located and brought to the surface the bodies of 11 of the miners who were caught below when the explosion ripped through the shaft.

"It was the beginning of the realization of the grim truth," Jobb says. "There was always hope until then. In these situations, people always cling to hope, but this was a sign of just how truly devastating this explosion had been."

For several more days, rescue crews and draegermen (rescue workers) who had come from other parts of the country to lend a hand made their way into the dark recesses of the mine—or of what was left of the shafts. It was dangerous work, and the men knew the risks, but in the brotherhood of miners, it was necessary. They knew that if the situation were reversed, these men would do the same for them.

On the surface, the confusion, frustration and anger continued to mount. The world's attention was now focused on this small community in Nova Scotia, Canada.

"This was now international news," Jobb recalls. "This was being flashed around the globe. The place was literally crawling with media from everywhere. As the days progressed, the tension mounted. You had the unusual situation where, in the community centre, all the media was set up with their satellite trucks trying to cover the story as best they could with little information, while right next door in the Plymouth fire hall, there were all the families huddled around, waiting for news of their loved ones, and they were all off limits to the reporters," he points out. "It was a tense situation at times."

Jobb says what stands out for him were images of the family hugging and hoping, crying and praying together. "The people were clinging to hope no matter how dire things became, even though I think people knew in their hearts that the chances of a miracle were not good. People have to believe as only people in those situations can."

Two days after the first 11 bodies were recovered, the remains of four more miners were located. Then, realizing the danger that rescue crews were facing, the company announced that it was terminating the search for the remaining missing men. Company officials confirmed that considering the force of the explosion, they believed there was no chance of any survivors below the surface and that sending rescue crews back down into the mine was just too risky.

With that, Jobb says, all hope was dashed. He says he remembers the dejected looks on the faces of family members upon hearing of the decision. "No hope was left," he recalls. "The company may have made what they thought was the best decision at the time, but they took away all the families' hope with that announcement."

The body of Glenn Martin was one of those left behind in the mine.

Allen Martin recalls that it was a difficult day for his family. "I think that's when we knew they were lost," he recalls. "When the company announced they were going to withdraw all rescue attempts we no longer had any hope...We knew that we had lost Glenn forever."

In hindsight, Allen says, the families probably should not have been surprised at the decision to end the search. "By that time, I'm sure we all knew what the reality was, but all you have is hope when you're faced with something like this. It's just too painful to let go."

After that announcement from the company, Allen said they had to face new realities. "At the point, we found ourselves asking, 'What do we do now? What comes next for us?'" he explains.

As news of the search being called off spread throughout the community, Jobb says all that hope turned to cynicism and criticism, and it was all directed at the company.

"People were coming forward and saying that it was known that the mine wasn't safe, that there were things going on down in that mine that have been going on for a very long time."

Clearly, Jobb says, people had held their tongues before the explosion for fear of losing their jobs, and there were people who kept quiet after the accident because of shock and guilt. "There were people who had booked off that night who could have been down there, or people who had just come off a shift. They understood it could have just as easily been them down in the mine when the explosion occurred. They were in no mood to talk about it, and they certainly wanted someone to pay for what had happened. Someone had to be held accountable."

It was later revealed that the miners expected, long before the explosion, that someday a tragedy such as this would happen. Jobb says, "They actually had it down to a lottery. Four crews worked down in the mine around the clock. They knew there was one in four chances it could be them. This information started coming out right after the search was called off."

In the weeks, months and years that followed, Jobb points out, there was a lot of blame to go around.

"The company was desperate to blame individual miners, management was desperate to blame anyone," he says:

> "The picture that emerged through media reports and investigations—and ultimately through RCMP investigations and the laying of criminal charges and finally through the provincial inquiry—was that there was no doubt this was a disaster waiting to happen and that it could have been prevented. Accident is not a good a word to describe this tragedy, because that word implies that nothing could have been done to prevent it. This was a totally preventable disaster. The mine was not run safely. That's a fact. The experts could quibble

over exactly what started the fire, but this was a work
site that was totally mismanaged in terms of safety."

Jobb lists off rudimentary safety rules that were not followed. "For example, according to labour laws, the miners weren't supposed to work 12-hour shifts. Westray ignored the rules and had the men work 12-hour shifts. How could the miners refuse?" Jobb asks. "The company was ordered to clean up the coal dust and to keep methane levels under control, but they didn't do it. If things like that had been done, who knows what would have happened?"

Allen Martin explains that the surviving family members endured difficult times. "In the days that followed the explosion, we could go to the community centre and check on progress, but after they called off the search, we were alone. What do you then? The people in the community were good to us, but we had no idea about what was coming or how to deal with it. There is no doubt that the men all died instantly down there. I believe that. All the rescue workers wanted to keep going until all the bodies were retrieved for the sake of the families, but it was just too dangerous. We understood that, but at first we didn't understand all the political fallout that was happening," he observes.

As Jobb goes on to say, there was plenty of fallout yet to come. "The mine was closed and 26 men were lost. Could anything positive come from such a tragedy? That's a good question," he says. "There was certainly a lot of frustration, there was a whole battle brewing between the inquiry and the criminal case. Charges under the Occupational Health and Safety Act that probably would have stuck were dropped in favour of a criminal case that subsequently fell apart during the trial. The inquiry went ahead, and if there was any measure of justice that came out of this, it was the fact that it finally came out that the mine was unsafe. It came out that it was not the responsibility of the individual miners, that they had been failed by the government regulations and that the mine management had failed them. That was really important, but the fact that nobody paid any kind of price for what had happened, that the head of the company could thumb his nose from Toronto and not ever come to testify, that just wasn't right."

Today, Jobb says, Nova Scotians can thank the Westray disaster for making their workplaces safer. "When we hear comments that safety inspectors today are being too rigid, I think that's a good thing. The Westray tragedy did lead to an overhaul of the health and safety regime in Nova Scotia, both from an enforcement perspective and from the law itself. We have updated mining regulations, although at the present time there are no longer any mines operating in Nova Scotia except for the salt mines in Pugwash. But the overall safety rules for all companies in Nova Scotia have been changed and modernized, and that's a good thing," he asserts. "That's important."

Westray, he says, has become a symbol for the rights and safety of workers in the province of Nova Scotia. "If there is a positive legacy to come out of Westray, that would be it. The feds have now criminalized workplace safety violations under the Criminal Code. One would hope that company managers don't need the law to tell them to do the right thing, but that's there now if it's needed," he continues. "Westray is really a symbol of what happens if you get a rogue company that basically thinks it can do whatever it wants."

Some people will carry Westray with them for the rest of lives, Jobb says. Certainly, that is the case for the families of the men who died in the blast. "Getting on with your life doesn't mean that it goes away. It brought a lot of people together through shared grief and loss. They'll always have that bond, but I think many of them are moving on and coping. They have no choice."

For Allen Martin and his family, the hurt will always be present, but they've come to terms with it. "My parents are strong Catholics, and it would mean a great deal to my mother to have her son buried in consecrated ground, but that's never going to happen. The mine site is closed and sealed, and we're living our lives, but of course we always keep Glenn's memory with us."

Becoming involved in the ensuing investigations and inquiry has also helped, he says. "Over the years, we've forced changes, and I do think things are much better now than it was back then, but the mindset is still the same, and that is to make profit at whatever cost. We live in a capitalist society, and that's what capitalism is—use people to make a profit," Allen notes. "We know we have to keep working at it to make sure this [kind of tragedy] never happens again."

Allen says he believes most family members have come to their own level of understanding of the tragedy on their own terms, in their own way. "It took a while, but I think most people are there now. It was a strain on the community and the province as a whole. The community responded so well. People in this area were absolutely amazing to us. They couldn't do enough for us. You've got to accept that life goes on and that you have to go on with it. If you don't, you're going to be ill. Somehow you have to pick up the pieces. It's tough at times, but you've got to do it," he admits.

Today, Allen says, because of Westray, Nova Scotian workers are more aware of their work environment and of their rights. "There have been changes in legislation. There is a lot of training taking place. There's the right to refuse to work if a worker feels unsafe. Upgraded mine regulations and a new occupational health and safety act have been implemented. I see that safety is now on everyone's mind. There is an awareness there now that wasn't there before Westray. To me, that's the Westray legacy."

Jobb sums it up this way:

> "Westray could have been safe. It was a viable mine. Instead, we lost 26 men. We lost all the direct and indirect jobs from the mine. We lost the resource and its value to the economy—the heartbreak and all the effort and millions of dollars spent to try to get to the bottom of this on RCMP probes and on the inquiry itself. Then there's the political cost. It's a ripple effect that we can't even begin to tabulate."

Justice K. Peter Richard led an inquiry into the disaster. In his report, entitled *The Westray Story, a Predictable Path to Disaster,* he found that the deaths of the 26 miners were the "catastrophic result" of failing to adhere to proper mining practices and procedures.

The report concluded that no matter how well spelled-out regulations are on paper, they are of no value if proper monitoring procedures are not in place and the regulations go unenforced. Justice Richard ultimately recommended more than 70 changes in legislation and provincial policy in an attempt to ensure that a Westray-type disaster does not occur again and that proper mining practices would be adhered to. In 1993, more than 50 noncriminal counts of failing to operate a safe mine were brought against the mine owners, but the company went bankrupt, and the case never made it to court. Based on the data available, Curragh Inc., the corporate entity that owned and operated Westray, and the individuals responsible for directing the facility were never brought to trial for criminal negligence causing death or manslaughter.

Timothy Hynes of the Faculty of Management at the University of Calgary, who was investigating Westray as part of his doctoral thesis, reported that the safety issues at Westray were the result of workers failing to follow basic regulations and management subsequently electing not to force compliance. A union head had apparently complained prophetically about the level of residual coal dust that workers had been operating in two months prior to the explosion, lamenting that the unsafe conditions at the mine would cause someone to lose his life.

Only 15 of the 26 bodies were ever recovered from the mine. The remaining 11 were sealed in the mine's southwest main shaft because of safety concerns. The land above the mine was levelled in 1998. In the process, two coal silos were imploded. In April 2002, the province sold the Westray site for $400,000.

Crash of Swissair Flight 111

September 2, 1998
St. Margaret's Bay, Nova Scotia

- **8:18 PM (EDT)**
  Swissair Flight 111 takes off from JFK International Airport in New York bound for Geneva with 215 passengers and 14 crew members on board

- **8:58 PM (EDT)**
  The MD-11 reaches cruising altitude of 10,000 metres

- **10:10 PM (ADT)**
  The flight crew detects an unusual odour in the cockpit

- **10:13 PM (ADT)**
  The pilots see smoke in the cockpit

- **10:14 PM (ADT)**
  The pilot declares "Pan-Pan, Pan-Pan, Pan-Pan," an international signal indicating that there is a problem with the aircraft

- **10:15 PM (ADT)**
  The decision is made to divert the jet to Halifax, and the plane begins its descent

- **10:20 PM (ADT)**
  The flight crew radios that they need to dump fuel before landing. Air traffic control clears the plane to turn south for a fuel dump

- **10:24 PM (ADT)**
  The autopilot disconnects, and the pilot informs the controller that he must fly manually. The flight data recorder begins to record aircraft system failures.

Flight 111 declares an emergency. The pilot radios that the plane is starting to dump fuel and must land immediately.

- 10:25 PM (ADT)
  The flight data recorder and cockpit voice recorder stop registering information

- 10:26 PM (ADT)
  Flight 111 disappears from radar screens at a last known altitude of 2900 metres

- 10:31 PM (ADT)
  The aircraft hits the water off Peggy's Cove, Nova Scotia, at 560 kilometres per hour. All 229 people on board are killed. Flight 111 plunged into the Atlantic with such force that it rattled nearby homes.

In Blandford, Nova Scotia, a tiny postcard-perfect hamlet on the province's rugged coastline, less than an hour's drive south of the capital city of Halifax, Marilyn Publicover and her husband, Lamont, had just settled down for the evening. It was after 10:00 PM on that dark, dreary September evening, and she thought a good book would help her fall asleep, so she snuggled into her warm, comfortable bed next to her husband with the book in hand. Marilyn had no sooner made herself comfortable when she heard a tremendous rumbling noise as it rolled over the house. The entire place vibrated. At first, she thought it was thunder.

Asking Lamont if he thought a storm was coming, she instinctively had a feeling that something was not right about the noise she had just heard.

"No," Lamont answered, getting out of bed and hurrying into his clothes. As a member of the local volunteer fire department, he knew that if something bad had just happened, he would soon be called for assistance. "I don't think so. That didn't sound like thunder."

Almost immediately, his pager began, the urgent voice spilling news of the tragedy into the quiet Publicover house. "All firefighters report immediately," the pager said, revealing the tragic news. "We have a report that a plane has gone down somewhere on the Aspotogan Peninsula."

Along with the Blandford department, firefighters from along the South Shore and the Halifax Metro region were now being dispatched to the St. Margaret's Bay area as news of the crash quickly spread throughout the region. Meanwhile, at the Publicover home, Marilyn had made her way to their deck, the scene of so many pleasant activities in the past. As she felt the night air on her skin, the quiet immediately embraced her, the eerie stillness making her uneasy. As she stood there in the damp fog of a late-summer night, she was immediately taken by the calmness. She noted that not even a breeze was blowing. Later, she would recall that at that moment she thought it was as if God had made the world stand still.

But the quiet was temporary. Within minutes, the sounds of screaming sirens from emergency crews cut through the night as fire trucks, police cars and ambulances sped past her house towards the suspected crash site. As the urgency increased, and everyone hoped for the best but feared the worst, the odour of jet fuel began wafting over the small community. Almost by an instinct that came with spending years as a firefighter's wife, Marilyn grabbed several blankets from a linen closet, threw other provisions into a cardboard box and headed to the nearby community centre. She knew that if something major had happened, rescue crews would need all the support they could get.

As she headed towards the centre, however, she could not even begin to imagine the magnitude of the events that were about to unfold within her beloved village.

It would be the second-worst air disaster ever to occur on Canadian territory, after the Gander crash 13 years earlier. There would be no survivors among the 229 passengers and crew members en route from New York to Geneva.

The flight had taken off from JFK International Airport at 9:18 PM local time. It carried a Saudi Arabian prince, well-known scientists, a renowned AIDS activist, United Nations officials, newlyweds, mothers, fathers, brothers, sisters, sons and daughters. The plane, a three-engine McDonnell Douglas MD-11, was travelling at approximately 10,000 metres when it passed over Liverpool, Nova Scotia, at 10:22 PM. At that time, the crew notified air traffic control in Moncton, New Brunswick, that there was smoke in the cockpit. Captain Urs Zimmermann and First Officer Stephan Loew requested an unscheduled landing, suggesting Boston, but they were diverted to Halifax because it was closer, only 130 kilometres compared to 560.

According to air traffic control recordings released after the tragedy by the Transportation Safety Board of Canada, when the crew learned a few minutes later that it was only 56 kilometres to the runway, they informed air traffic control that they needed more distance. The plane was still travelling at between 4570 and 5500 metres. At that point, Flight 111 turned towards the north, then announced that it needed to dump fuel before it could land. The MD-11 has a maximum landing weight of 195 tonnes, but the plane at that point weighed 230 tonnes because it still had most of the fuel needed to get to Europe.

With directions from air traffic control, Flight 111 continued its turn and headed south over St. Margaret's Bay
on the southern coast of Nova Scotia, preparing to dump
fuel. At 10:24 PM, the crew radioed: "We are declaring an
emergency...we have to land immediately."

That was the last communication from Flight 111.
Radar tracked the aircraft for a further six minutes as it
turned towards the west, made a complete circle in
a southeasterly direction and disappeared.

Residents all along Nova Scotia's South Shore reported
hearing a low-flying aircraft followed by a reverberating
bang. Some people on the Aspotogan Peninsula near
Halifax reported that a crash had shaken their homes
around 10:30 PM.

Local fishermen were the first to take to the water to
search for the downed passenger plane, quickly followed
by the RCMP, Coast Guard, military ships and aircraft.
The search continued until debris was subsequently
located about 8 kilometres southwest of the world-famous
Peggy's Cove, a few kilometres off the small island of East
Ironbound, at around 12:30 AM. Despite a massive rescue
operation that went on through the remainder of that
early morning, day and night and into the next day, by
Friday officials said all hope of finding survivors was gone.
Swissair had already announced that no one had lived
through the disaster, and rescue officials now agreed.

The focus then switched from search and rescue to
search and recovery as more Canadian Navy and Coast
Guard vessels moved in to help recover debris and
remains. The RCMP began calling the area a crime scene,
and the Coast Guard imposed a no-shipping and no-fly
zone from Mahone Bay to Chebucto Head.

Early numbers released indicated that 60 bodies had
been recovered, but officials refused to say any more, citing
humanitarian reasons and difficulties with identification.

Millions of pieces of the wrecked jet were recovered from the
bottom of the Atlantic Ocean and taken to a nearby naval base.
Some of the debris can be seen here, under guard by RCMP and
other authorities.

~∞X∞~

Almost from the time the first crash debris was discovered, reports from fishermen and searchers indicated that
body parts were found scattered among small bits of
debris covering over 700 square kilometres of the Atlantic
and washed up along the Nova Scotia coast. The largest
piece of the wreckage found by Saturday was no bigger
than a car roof.

With the changed focus of what was now being called
Operation Persistence, additional vessels and searchers were
called in. Over the weekend, nine Canadian Navy and five
Coast Guard vessels, led by HMCS *Preserver*, were in the St.
Margaret's Bay area. Over 1500 soldiers, sailors and air-
men were involved in the recovery effort, along with the

RCMP (some 380 officers were divided between recovery and victim identification efforts), other government agencies and volunteers, including local ground search and rescue teams. Hundreds of other volunteers provided everything from grief counselling to boxed lunches.

As the RCMP were continuing to sift through boxes containing millions of pieces of collected debris at CFB Shearwater near Halifax, analyzing everything for evidence of a bomb, officials said there was no indication the crash had resulted from terrorism.

That finding was echoed by the province's chief medical examiner, Dr. John Butt, who was overseeing efforts to identify the victims of Flight 111. Dr. Butt said the remains collected indicated impact injuries—not drowning, toxic fumes or an explosion—caused the deaths. Only one body, that of a French woman, had been identified by that time.

Vic Gerden, the chief accident investigator heading up a team of 40 investigators from the Transportation Safety Board, along with an equal number of additional representatives from the United States, Switzerland and other countries, said the cause of the accident would not be known for some time. Investigators were looking into all aspects of the crash, reviewing information on aircraft specifications and maintenance along with human performance by the crew and all those associated with Flight 111. But it is information gleaned from the flight data recorder and cockpit voice recorder, the famous black boxes, that would help investigators the most.

The flight data recorder, which maintains records of more than 100 parameters associated with the plane's operation, was recovered Sunday afternoon, two days after the crash, and flown to a Transportation Safety Board lab in Ottawa. But Gerden announced the following day that it had stopped recording at 10:25 PM, when the plane was still at 3000 metres, giving no information about the last six minutes of Flight 111. However, he noted that it would still be useful to the investigation, because it provided data about what was happening up to that point. Experts said the implication was that the plane had suffered electrical failure. Early in the investigation, Gerden suggested that those faults might eventually be traced to a common problem. Regarding the cockpit voice recorder, which captures conversation among the flight crew as well as mechanical noises in the aircraft, Gerden said even if the recorder was retrieved from the ocean floor intact, Canadian law prohibits the public release of transcripts taken from it.

"In Canada, recorded cockpit voice recorder information is used strictly for the purpose of advancing transportation safety, and there are tight restrictions on access to it and its use," he told a media briefing. He said, though, that some factual information might be released to "facilitate understanding."

During the first week following the crash, sea efforts continued to focus on the retrieval of that second black box and human remains. By Monday, the Canadian Navy submarine HMCS *Okanagan* had detected the signal from the cockpit voice recorder, and divers attempted to locate it. Officials admitted, however, that an electrical failure on the aircraft could have caused that black box to stop recording as well. Based on the recordings from the air traffic control centre, the investigators believed the pilots were wearing oxygen masks, but they knew little else about the plane's situation at this point.

"We really don't have enough information to determine the conditions inside the cockpit of the airplane. Really, we don't know what density of smoke, what amount of smoke," Gerden told reporters at the time.

However, he defended the pilot's decision to turn away from the airport, despite being only some 55 kilometres away, because the plane was still too high and too heavy with fuel.

"It was certainly a difficult situation to contend with," the chief investigator said. "If one attempts to land an aircraft at a weight that is greater than the maximum landing weight... there is a risk that having landed the aircraft, it would go off the end at the other end of the runway at some unknown rate of speed and cause damage."

In another major development, officials announced that three large pieces believed to be part of the aircraft's fuselage were located in about 50 metres of water near the suspected crash site. They were not sitting in a straight line and were spread over quite an area. "Some of them are squashed. It's in very poor shape, but it is visible and it looks like an aircraft fuselage," Navy Captain Phil Webster said at the time.

The salvage and rescue ship USS *Grapple* was dispatched from Philadelphia to lift those sections of the aircraft. (This vessel had been used to recover sections of TWA Flight 800, which had crashed near New York in July 1996, and would the following year participate in the Egypt Air recovery off Nantucket.) But first, a number of dead believed to still be strapped in their seats would have to be recovered. Divers went down with body bags to retrieve them.

Swissair's response to the tragedy was immediate. In addition to being the first to announce that there were no survivors, the company quickly offered to fly family members of Flight 111's passengers and crew to Nova Scotia to view the crash scene. Delta Airlines, which had 53 passengers and one flight attendant on board this shared flight, echoed the offer. The first Swissair airbus carrying family of the victims touched down at Halifax

International Airport within days of the crash, and family members began making the first of many pilgrimages to Peggy's Cove, the normally thriving tourist destination turned search command centre.

When they came, the mourners brought flowers and teddy bears. They stood on the rocks and looked out to sea. Some openly wept, and some prayed. Some took bottles of water away from the Atlantic as memories of loved ones claimed in the crash. A few bought postcards of the famous lighthouse, which had become a sad beacon of the tragedy. Away from Peggy's Cove, the families cooperated with the investigation. They identified personal belongings gathered in the salvage operation and gave DNA samples to match with victims' remains.

Officials continued to promise that the search wouldn't end until all hope of finding their loved ones was gone. "We will not spare any efforts or time to find all of the bodies or remains," RCMP spokesman Sergeant Andre Guertin said in a news conference. "We are resolved to continue until we are satisfied we have everything."

Two Canadians were among those who died aboard Flight 111. Yves de Roussan was a Geneva-based European advisor for UNICEF from Montréal. He was 41 and left behind a wife and three children. George Abady, 24, from Toronto was on his way to Geneva to attend a hotel management conference. The list of passengers by country of residence included 136 Americans, 30 French, 28 Swiss, 6 British, 3 Germans, 3 Italians, 2 Greeks and one each from Saudi Arabia, Yugoslavia, Afghanistan, Iran, Spain, St. Kitts and Russia. One of the flight attendants was on her first flight. The pilot, Captain Zimmermann, died just three days before he would have celebrated his 50th birthday.

A postcard of Peggy's Cove hung on Peggy Coburn's refrigerator when Swissair Flight 111 made her a widow.

She and her husband, Richard, had moved several times since her aunt had visited Nova Scotia seven years ago and sent her that memento, but somehow the card had always gone back up. What an eerie coincidence that her husband died in a place her aunt encouraged them to visit.

The tragedy off Nova Scotia's South Shore in September 1998 left Peggy a widow at 38, raising three young children on her own. It happened less than two weeks after she and her husband celebrated their 10th anniversary. When she came to Nova Scotia two days after the crash, Peggy didn't know what to expect. She wasn't even sure why she'd come, half afraid to get on an airplane and risk leaving her children orphans. It was a bereavement counsellor who convinced her to travel to where Richard perished with the other 228 souls late on the night of September 2.

When she came, Peggy had two thoughts in mind—she was bringing her husband's dental records to aid the identification of his remains, and she wanted to take some sand from the shore back home with her. What she found was almost a miracle. Peggy said it was in Nova Scotia that she found the strength to go on, the will to make a life for herself and her children without Richard.

"Every person that I met here, every single person, was so concerned about me. They were concerned about all of us," Peggy told Lighthouse Publishing reporter Lisa Brown in December 1998. "It was person to person. They really cared. It literally gave me strength to have people reaching out to me. It really transformed me."

From the fishermen who put out to sea in the stormy night to search in vain for survivors of the crash to the salvage workers who conducted the grim recovery work—even the kind and compassionate bus drivers and hotel employees—amazed Peggy. They weren't simply polite in the face of the families' grief, they shared it from the bottoms of their hearts. "I realized that the world is teeming with really good people," she said. "What a gruesome scene, and they were willing to put themselves through that for me and for other people—out of love. It was so incredibly powerful. Words like 'thank you' don't mean nearly what I feel. It's wrong to sum it up in two words."

Peggy's sister, Ronnie Newman, who had accompanied the New Jersey woman and her 10-month-old daughter, Alia, to Nova Scotia, told reporter Brown that she believed her sister was coping well with the tragedy and agreed that she had found a source of strength here.

"I have a feeling that's part of the reason why this is where the plane went down. Part of the reason was to provide that to us, to allow us to heal," Ronnie said, describing her brother-in-law as a kind and fair man who was both artistic and intelligent. "He was very patient and unconditionally accepting of people. He was like an anchor. Peggy used to call him the anchor."

Richard was on a business trip when he died. He'd never been to Nova Scotia, but his wife was certain that he would have loved it here. "From the beginning I've always wanted his grave to be here. It just feels right," Peggy said. "It's so beautiful, but the people add to that. To me, the people make it almost more than beautiful—it's almost holy or blessed."

Peggy said she felt a spiritual connection to the South Shore brought about in part by a series of uncanny coincidences beyond the postcard. There's her name and the link to Peggy's Cove. She and Richard weren't religious people, but she said when they discussed spirituality, her husband told her if he could ever commune with God, it wouldn't be inside a sanctuary, but outside on

The famous lighthouse at Peggy's Cove was the background for one of the worst aviation disasters in Canadian history.

a mountain. When she went rummaging through a box of photographs before her husband's memorial service following the crash, one of the first she picked up was a photo of Richard standing on a mountain. The rocks, Peggy said, greatly resembled those of Peggy's Cove, and she chose that photo for the service.

During a return trip to Nova Scotia in 1999 to participate in a memorial service for the victims of Swissair Flight 111, Peggy told Brown that she needed to tell Nova Scotians what they had done for her, how they had given her strength and comfort to move on with her life. "All I need to do is remember, and it's there forever. What a gift," she said.

Peggy's experience in Nova Scotia changed her life, particularly in the way she saw her fellow humans. Even while going through a grocery check-out in New York City where she lived, she said she viewed the clerk in a new way—as a person who sleeps in a bed and brushes her teeth and lives a life beyond what Peggy and other shoppers could see.

Of the recovery efforts in Nova Scotia, Peggy said:

"It gave me a lot of peace that anyone who might be handling Richard's remains or his things, it was okay, it was being done with love. I could really relax. That was really important to tell them and how it changed me as far as me feeling connected to people. What they did was beyond heroic. When you save someone's life, you're a hero. When they went out to save lives, they were on their way to becoming heroes. And when there was no one to save and they continued to work, they were really superheroes, because there was no reward. They were just, without knowing me or Richard or the family members of the other victims, they were loving us and doing something really incredible for us."

Blandford resident Marilyn Publicover stands besides the memorial erected at Bayswater Beach on Nova Scotia's South Shore. The granite memorial lists the names of all those people who died in the Swissair crash.

~ひ⌘~

The year following the disaster was not easy, Peggy admitted to Brown. "I'd give anything to have him back, but I vowed that I will live my life as a tribute to him, so I have to be really good now. It would only be right for me to live my life and enjoy my life and try really hard to move forward and live the best life I can. He would want that for me."

It helps that she knows Richard died happy. The epitaph on his grave is *carpe diem* (seize the day). It's the way they lived and the way they made important decisions. "He died with no regrets," she said. "There was nothing that he wanted to try, no dream that he wanted to go after that he didn't move toward."

Peggy said she was content because part of her husband will remain in Nova Scotia, a place he would have loved. When she visits Nova Scotia, she stays in Blandford with Lamont and Marilyn Publicover. Now they are like a second family to her.

"They were such warm, nice, loving, sharing people that I just felt totally connected to them. I'll never just drift away from them. I feel a very strong connection," she said.

For Peggy's brother, Fred Newman, Nova Scotia is equally important. It was here, he said, through the goodness of the people that he came to believe in God. He had come to Nova Scotia with Peggy in September 1998 following Richard's death. He had laid flowers in the water at Peggy's Cove as she watched, but he found himself almost overcome by his own grief. He had started to cry but forced himself to stop. "I was supposed to be her rock," he recalled.

A rabbi had told him to go ahead and weep, but Fred explained that he couldn't because his sister needed him the be strong. A Mountie standing nearby had overheard the conversation.

"All of a sudden, somebody taps me on the shoulder. I turn around and it's this big, strapping policeman, the kind of person you want to have as a cop," Fred remembered. "As I turn around, there are four of them, and they have their arms around each other, blocking between me and my two sisters. They turn to me and they say to me, 'Your sister can't see you now. It's okay to cry.' I'm going to take that to my grave with me."

Frequently hampered by the weather, search crews spent months recovering debris and human remains from the disaster site. Seven Canadian Navy and seven Coast

Guard ships continued to work on Operation Persistence. The RCMP Patrol Vessel *Simmonds* joined the team to act as a floating detachment for the eight smaller RCMP boats involved in the salvage effort. After three months, the command ship HMCS *Preserver* was replaced by the HMCS *Halifax*, which was assigned to Operation Persistence for three weeks, though work off the South Shore was to last longer than that.

The hundreds of military, Coast Guard auxiliaries and ground search and rescue volunteers combed the beaches of St. Margaret's and Mahone Bays, collecting debris washed ashore. Through the hard work and ingenuity of both the sea- and land-based sections of the salvage team, all but 2 percent of the plane, including over 250 kilometres of wire, was eventually recovered.

A week after the crash, the province's chief medical examiner, Dr. John Butt, announced the identification of two more bodies from dental records, bringing the total identifications to four of the 229 people on board the aircraft.

Canadian Prime Minister Jean Chrétien and Swiss President Flavio Cotti visited Peggy's Cove following a September 9 memorial service at nearby Indian Harbour. Canada's prime minister expressed sympathy for the family members of the victims and appreciation for the workers and volunteers.

"I just want to express my thanks to the people of the area for what they've done. I think they've been fantastic, and I've received comments from the United States and France and Switzerland for the dedication and commitment and generosity of the people of this area," Chrétien said. "On behalf of the Government of Canada, I want to thank all those involved."

In March 2003, almost four and a half years later, a report from the Transportation Safety Board (TSB) concluded that, when a fire started in the ceiling above the cockpit of Swissair Flight 111 on September 2, 1998, the people on board the jet had no chance of survival. That conclusion came with the release of the board's final report into the disaster. More than 300 pages detail the series of dangers and deficiencies on the MD-11 that made it impossible for the pilots to have had any chance of landing safely.

The plane had been travelling at 10,000 metres when the flight crew first detected an unusual odour in the cockpit at 10:10 PM. Three minutes later, they saw smoke. By the time the pilots realized there was a serious problem, conditions were deteriorating quickly, and aircraft systems began to fail. Flames burned through the ceiling, and the cockpit filled with heat and smoke.

"Because of the rapid progression of the fire, they would not have been able to complete a safe landing in Halifax," chief investigator Gerden told a Halifax news conference on March 27, 2003. Calling the crash "a wake-up call" for the aviation industry, Mr. Gerden reviewed the details that led to the crash into the Atlantic off Peggy's Cove at 10:31 PM.

The fire above the cockpit ceiling began when a wire supplying power to the controversial in-flight entertainment system apparently arced. That system, added after the plane was built, allowed passengers in the business- and first-class sections to gamble, play video games and watch movies in their seats.

The investigators believe that that spark likely led to further arcing in other nearby wires, igniting flammable coverings on surrounding insulation blankets. TSB tests showed the blankets ignited easily and caused the fire to spread rearwards into the attic area above the front passenger cabin.

"It is important to emphasize here, that without the presence of this and other flammable material, this accident would not have happened," Gerden said at the time.

Although the investigators were highly critical of the flammable insulation blankets, they stopped short of squarely blaming the in-flight entertainment system. Gerden said it is "unlikely" that its power supply wire was the only wire involved in the initial arcing.

Investigators found 20 pieces of wire that showed signs of arcing from amid the more than 250 kilometres of wire on the plane. "We strongly suspect that at least one other wire was involved, either an aircraft wire or another wire from the entertainment system," he said. "However, we were unable to identify or place any of the other arced wires in the area where we believe the fire originated." Incidentally, had the plane's circuit breakers been of an improved design, they could have stopped the arcing before a fire occurred.

Because the odour and smoke initially moved forwards into the cockpit through a panel near an air-conditioning outlet, the pilots believed the air-conditioning system was responsible. Such situations are not uncommon and are usually benign, so the crew did not initially perceive a serious threat. Gerden said there were no warnings on the pilots' panels to indicate problems with the electrical systems. There was no requirement to have smoke or fire detectors, which could have provided critical information, installed above the cockpit or cabin ceiling. As the pilots worked their way through an emergency checklist, they turned off most of the power to the passenger cabin. When air recirculation fans above the cabin ceiling stopped, the expanding fire was drawn forwards into the attic above the cockpit. A short time later, the pilots declared an emergency, and systems began to fail.

The legacy of the $57 million Swissair probe is found
in 23 safety recommendations. Together, they are
intended to:

- reduce the risks associated with thermal acous-
  tic insulation materials and ensure appropriate
  testing before new materials are certified

- ensure add-on systems, such as the in-flight
  entertainment system on Swissair, are properly
  analyzed

- establish an industry standard for circuit breaker
  function

- improve the quality of cockpit voice recorder
  recordings

- require new aircraft to record more flight data

- install image recording systems in cockpits

- harmonize international rules for the protec-
  tion of cockpit voice and image recordings for
  safety investigations.

Following interim recommendations from the board,
flammable thermal insulation blankets were removed
from the 700 United States aircraft that had them. No
aircraft in Canada needed the modification, but 1900
additional aircraft around the world did. Gerden said the
United States Federal Aviation Administration (FAA)
issued more than 50 airworthiness directives to elimi-
nate potential fire sources aboard MD-11 aircraft.

The TSB also called for improved inflight firefighting
measures, including built-in detection and suppression
equipment. Swissair voluntarily disconnected the in-
flight entertainment system, unique to its airline, from
its other planes following the crash. The United States
FAA later banned its use and ordered changes to 18 systems with similar shortcomings.

Speaking to international media on March 27, 2003, TSB chairman Camille Thériault called the Swissair probe the "largest, most complex" investigation ever conducted by the TSB. "We can take some consolation in knowing that much has been learned from this investigation—and that many measures have already been taken to enhance aviation safety today—and well into the future," he said.

Thériault observed that the investigation was made easier by the assistance and cooperation of many people, from those who worked to understand the crash to those who put their lives on hold to assist the victims' families. He thanked the people of Nova Scotia, particularly those living in communities surrounding the crash site, one last time, saying, "In the darkest days, you provided comfort where there was only pain; compassion where there was only suffering; hope where there was only despair. Thank you for showing the world the very best of our national character."

The residents of Nova Scotia's South Shore near the crash site will never look at the ocean again in the same way. On that stormy evening of September 2, 1998, they watched in growing horror as emergency vehicles screamed along the shoreline. They witnessed the lights of fishing boats as they headed out on raging waves to look for survivors. Then came the terrible news that all 229 people aboard the flight en route from New York to Geneva had perished. In the days and months that followed, the residents heard horrifying stories and watched as workers combed the shores along St. Margaret's Bay in an endless effort to retrieve human remains and wreckage from the jetliner.

Marilyn Publicover, whose early involvement with the disaster response was described earlier, was the municipal councillor for the area when Flight 111 crashed off the coast. In the rush that followed that fateful night, the Blandford woman helped in little ways by preparing food and in bigger ways by being a surrogate family, with the help of her husband, for people who lost loved ones in the disaster. Although many people in the community wish for closure, if not to forget the crash, at least to stop talking and hearing about it, Marilyn doesn't think that's possible.

"I don't think it's something that's ever going to go away. Personally, I think there's no closure," she says. "The families [of the Flight 111 victims] will always feel that this a place to come to pay respects to their loved ones. In future years, I think fewer people and fewer families will come, but there will always be some who will come," she adds.

Marilyn goes on to explain that they don't come looking for pity. They travel here because they feel close to those they lost and to the people of Nova Scotia who welcomed and supported them in their grief.

"They're looking just for hugs and people just to say we're there for them. And they're thanking us," Marilyn says. "It's still fresh in people's minds after all these years. How could anyone ever forget something like this?"

Notes on Sources

Yankee Gale
The *Island Register.* "The Yankee Gale of 1851: From the collection of T.W. Stewart." http://www.islandregister. com/yankeegale.html

Saxby Gale
Bonvie, Marilyn. "The Saxby Gale of 1869." http:// www.rootsweb.com/~nbcharlo/saxby1.htm

Environment Canada, Canadian Hurricane Centre. http://www.atl.ec.gc.ca/weather/hurricane/hurricanes5. html

The United States National Oceanic and Atmospheric Administration. http://www.noaa.gov/

Raging Storms of the 1870s
DesBrisay, Mather B. *History of the County of Lunenburg* (2nd ed.). Toronto: William Briggs, 1895.

Environment Canada's Online Atlantic Climate Centre. "The Climate of Nova Scotia: a Meteorological Moment." http://atlantic-web1.ns.ec.gc.ca/climatecentre/default. asp?lang=En&n=61405176-1

The United States National Oceanic and Atmospheric Administration. http://www.noaa.gov/

Interview: David Phillips, senior climatologist with Environment Canada, Toronto, Ontario.

Hurricane Juan&White Juan

Environment Canada."2003 Tropical Cyclone Season Summary." http://www.atl.ec.gc.ca/weather/hurricane/storm03.html

Environment Canada. "Atlantic Canada Severe Weather Awareness." http://www.atl.ec.gc.ca/weather/severe/2003-2004/whitejuan_e.html

Fogarty, Chris. "Hurricane Juan Storm Summary." http://www.novaweather.net/Hurricane_Juan_files/Juan_Summary.pdf

Sinking of the *Titanic* (The Halifax Connection)

Hunston, Robert. Wireless Log: "The Titanic Disaster as Viewed from Cape Race." http://titanic.gov.ns.ca/wireless.html

The Maritime Museum of the Atlantic. http://titanic.gov.ns.ca/museum.html

Interview: Richard MacMichael, coordinator of visitor services and a senior interpreter at the Maritime Museum of the Atlantic, Halifax, Nova Scotia.

Great August Gales

The Fisheries Museum of the Atlantic, Lunenburg, Nova Scotia.

Lighthouse Publishing Ltd. http://www.lighthouse.ns.ca/

Interview: Ralph Getson, curator at the Fisheries Museum of the Atlantic, Lunenburg, Nova Scotia.

Newfoundland Tsunami

Library and Archives Canada, "S.O.S. Canadian Disasters: Water." http://www.collectionscanada.ca/sos/002028-1100-e.html

University of Washington Department of Earth Sciences,
"Tsunami: 1929 Grand Banks Tsunami." http://www.
ess.washington.edu/tsunami/index.html

Interview: Robert Parsons, historian, author and retired
schoolteacher, St. John's, Newfoundland.

Escuminac Salmon Disaster
Lunenburg *Progress-Enterprise,* June 24, 1959, courtesy of
the Miramichi *County Crier* http://www.inmgroup.net/
countycrier/countycriercom/id21.html

The United States National Oceanic and Atmospheric
Administration. http://www.noaa.gov/

Interviews: Brian Lloyd, Garth Williston, Captain Theodore
Williston and Walter Williston, survivors, Escuminac
region, New Brunswick.

Bell Island Boom
Bearden, T.E. "Historical Background of Scalar EM
Weapons." http://www.cheniere.org/books/analysis/
history.htm

Bell Island community website, "Bell Island: a History of
Bell Island." http://www.bellisland.net/tourist/history.
htm

Memorial University of Newfoundland, "Iron Ore Mines
of Bell Island: Newfoundland and Labrador Heritage."
http://www.heritage.nf.ca/society/bellisland_mines.
html

Sinking of the *Ocean Ranger*
The Canadian Broadcasting Corporation. "The Ocean
Ranger Disaster: Disasters and Tragedies." http://
archives.cbc.ca/IDCC-1-70-349/disasters_tragedies/
ocean_ranger/

Clarenville High School Social Studies GrassRoots Projects. "The *Ocean Ranger*." http://www.chs.k12.nf.ca/soc-stud/ssgrassroots/oceanranger/OceanRangerIntro.htm

Interviews: Brian Bursey, victim's brother, St. John's, Newfoundland; Samantha Gerbeau, victim's daughter, St. John's, Newfoundland.

Great Ice Storm of 1998
Environment Canada. "Ice Storm of 1998." http://www.msc-smc.ec.gc.ca/media/icestorm98/index_e.cfm

Miramichi Fire
Lambert, R.S. *Redcoat Sailor*. "Charlotte Taylor: Her Life and Times." http://www3.bc.sympatico.ca/charlotte_taylor/Folder1/Miramichi_Fire_of_1825.htm

Library and Archives Canada. "The Miramichi Fire of 1825: Sifting Through the Ashes at the National Library of Canada." http://www.collectionscanada.ca/bulletin/015017-0502-03-e.html

Interview: Manford Wasson, retired schoolteacher and president of the Miramichi Historical Society, Miramichi, New Brunswick.

Great Saint John Fire (Black Wednesday)
Trueman, Mac. Collected works from the *Telegraph-Journal*. http://new-brunswick.net/Saint_John/greatfire/greatfire.html

Great Commercial Street Fire
Hirtle, Patrick. *Going Against the Grain: The Rise of Bridgewater, Nova Scotia, 1812–1899*. (unpublished thesis).

Halifax Explosion
The Canadian Broadcasting Corporation. "The Halifax Explosion." http://www.cbc.ca/halifaxexplosion/

"On December 6th, 1917, History Was Changed Forever." http://www.halifaxexplosion.org/dayof.html

Interview: Gertrude Roy, survivor, Liverpool, Nova Scotia.

St. John's Knights of Columbus Hall Fire
McNaughton, Janet. "Knights of Columbus Hostel Fire." http://www.janetmcnaughton.ca/fire.html

St. John's *Evening Telegram*

Interview: Robert Parsons, historian, author and retired schoolteacher, St. John's, Newfoundland.

Nova Scotia's Mining Disasters
Cape Breton Miners' Museum. http://www.miners-museum.com/

Springhill Mine Disaster (The Explosion)
The Canadian Broadcasting Corporation. "Springhill Mining Disasters." http://archives.cbc.ca/IDD-1-70-111/disasters_tragedies/springhill/

Library and Archives Canada. "S.O.S. Canadian Disasters: Earth, Springhill Mining Disasters." http://www.collectionscanada.ca/sos/002028-2100-e.html

Public Archives of Nova Scotia. "Place-Names and Places of Nova Scotia."

Interviews: Dr. Arnold Burden, rescuer and author, Springhill, Nova Scotia; Ken Melanson, survivor, Springhill, Nova Scotia.

Springhill Mine Disaster (The Bump)
The Canadian Broadcasting Corporation. "Springhill Mining Disasters." http://archives.cbc.ca/IDD-1-70-111/disasters_tragedies/springhill/

Library and Archives Canada. "SOS! Canadian Disasters: Earth, Springhill Mining Disasters." http://www.collectionscanada.ca/sos/002028-2100-e.html

Public Archives of Nova Scotia. "Place-Names and Places of Nova Scotia."

Interviews: Dr. Arnold Burden, rescuer and author, Springhill, Nova Scotia; Caleb Rushton, survivor, Springhill, Nova Scotia.

Crash of Arrow Air Flight 1285
The Gander *Beacon*. via www.ganderbeacon.ca

Rowan, Roy. *Time Magazine*, "Gander—Different Crash, Same Questions." http://www.time.com/time/magazine/article/0,9171,975391,00.html

United States Department of the Army, *Historical Summary, FY 1986:* Appendix A, "Tragedy at Gander." http://www.army.mil/cmh/books/DAHSUM/1986/appA.htm

Interview: Greg Seward, former reporter and photographer at the Gander *Beacon*, Gander, Newfoundland.

Westray Mine Explosion
Westray Mine Disaster Index. http://www.littletechshoppe.com/ns1625/wraymenu.html

Interviews: Dean Jobb, investigative journalist and author, Halifax, Nova Scotia; Allen Martin, victim's brother, Stellarton, Nova Scotia.

Crash of Swissair Flight 111
Lighthouse Publishing Ltd. http://www.lighthouse.ns.ca/

Interviews: Lisa Brown, reporter, Lighthouse Publishing Ltd., Bridgewater, Nova Scotia; Marilyn Publicover, former municipal councillor and victim outreach supporter, Blandford, Nova Scotia.

～◯◯～

Vernon Oickle

Vernon Oickle was born in Liverpool, Nova Scotia, where he still lives with his wife and two sons. He has 25 years experience in the weekly newspaper business and has won numerous awards for writing and photography. Today, he is the editor of the *Bridgewater Bulletin* and is the author of seven books.

More stories of Canadian Disasters from Folklore Publishing...

Disasters of Ontario
75 Stories of Courage & Chaos

Ontario's history has been marked with disasters from which have emerged some of the most courageous stories. This book chronicles some of the most devastating events, from shipping and railway tragedies, tornadoes and hurricanes, to epidemics, environmental catastrophes and more. Read the personal stories of the province's darkest days and their human and environmental costs.

Softcover • 5.25" X 8.25" • 256 pages
ISBN13: 978-1-894864-14-5
ISBN10: 1-894864-14-X
$18.95

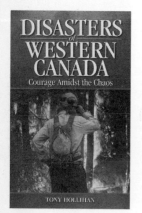

Disasters of Western Canada
Courage Amidst the Chaos

Great tragedies have struck the West, brought by the raging forces of nature and the accidental folly of humanity. The devastation, loss of life and courage in the face of adversity make for powerful and poignant stories. Read some of the most powerful tales of these chaotic events in BC, Alberta, Saskatchewan, Manitoba and the Yukon.

Softcover • 5.25" X 8.25" • 240 pages
ISBN13: 978-1-894864-13-8
ISBN10: 1-894864-13-1
$14.95

Available from your local bookseller or by contacting the distributor
Lone Pine Publishing
1-800-518-3541
www.lonepinepublishing.com